CHOOSING

THE

POSITIVE

FROM BELVEDERE TO BUDAPEST

via BALLYMOTE, BOSTON and IIB BANK

with best wishes,

Paddy McEvoy

Paddy McEvoy

Paperback ISBN: 978-1-911131-12-0

A CIP catalogue record for this book is available from
the National Library.

Edited by A&A Farmar
Cover Design by Sheila Hanley
Printed by Choice Publishing, Drogheda, Co Louth

"Believe it is possible to solve your problem. Tremendous things happen to the believer. So believe the answer will come. It will."

Norman Vincent Peale

All proceeds from the sale of this book
are being donated to:
The Belvedere Youth Club
Buckingham Street
Dublin

Table of Contents

Acknowledgements

The inspiration to write this memoir 'miraculously' occurred when I was lying in a hospital bed in Santa Cruz, the capital city of the beautiful island of Tenerife. I had spent 10 days there in considerable pain and awaiting invasive surgery. Being unable to do anything except stare at the ceiling I reflected on my life, on my positivity, and on all the good fortune and bounty that God had granted me. Writing this book has been a challenge but it was always a labour of love. I made new friends and re-engaged with old friends.

Writing a memoir is above all a journey of self-exploration and I am so grateful to all who have helped me in this endeavour. A very special thanks is due to my wife Keyna, who was a huge support to me in very practical ways and at all stages. Keyna and I shared the journey described in the memoir. My two sons, Redmond and Dermot, were a great help and encouragement to me, reviewing early drafts, proofreading and critiquing my work.

I am indebted to so many friends for all their support, advice and encouragement, including former colleagues from IIB Bank, particularly John Kelly, who read and advised on early drafts. Also to Ted Marah, John Reynolds, Christine Moran and Austin Hughes; they all brought back memories of a shared past. Special thanks is also due to our friends Gregory and Iris Park, both published authors in their own right. Fellow past Belvederians contributed generously of their time and talent particularly including, Gerry Walsh KSG, P.J. McAllister and Frank Young.

I am very grateful to Katherine Zappone and Anne Louise Gilligan for taking the time to read early drafts and for their wise counsel and encouragement. I am also grateful to Tony and Anna of A&A Farmar, not just for editing but also for sharing their wisdom and experience with me. I want to express my gratitude to Michael O'Brien of O'Brien Press and also to Brian Gilsenan of C.J. Fallon. A special thanks is due to a wonderful man, Martin Coffey, himself an experienced author, who gave so unselfishly in helping me bring this book to fruition. It would not have happened without him. And finally, my thanks to Choice Publishing and Book Services Ltd, Drogheda for their professionalism in the printing and completion of this book.

Prologue

As a career banker I am saddened and embarrassed by what has happened in recent years to the Irish Banking system. When I started out as a bank clerk with the Hibernian Bank back in 1957 bankers took pride in their profession; the focus was on customers and great satisfaction was to be had in providing services to the community. In recent times a new culture emerged when our industry effectively forgot or downgraded its traditional role in the pursuit of short-term profitability. And this has led to the complete breakdown of trust between banks, their customers and the community at large.

The party is well over now but its painful legacy remains with us. There is a broad consensus about what went wrong; we have had apologies, *mea culpa*s and the occasional denial. Niall FitzGerald, Executive Chairman of Unilever and a former director of the Bank of Ireland, during the 1990s, posed the question to the boards of Irish banks, asking them were they aware of the risks that were being taken and thus *'Complicit with the recklessness'*? Or were they unaware of what was going on and thus failing to discharge their responsibilities as directors. The Honohan report concurred, placing a major responsibility with the directors and senior management of the banks that got into trouble.

My story is of one man's journey from the early 1940's to the present day. And it is a reflection on how choosing the positives and taking advantage of life's opportunities can lead to good fortune and self-fulfilment. It is an acknowledgement of my debt to Belvedere College and the Jesuits as the great influence on my life philosophy and life choices. It is a love story and a social history. And it is also a journey and reflection on how the Irish banks morphed from being customer oriented, conservative, dull, and profoundly honest in the 1950's to the very different cultural profile seen in recent years.

Family photograph, September 2007 on the occasion of my Ph.D. conferral at University College Dublin. From left Anne, Redmond, Keyna, Paddy, Dermot, Rory, Hilda and in the front from left Sophie, Emma, Kate and Anna.

Dedication

This book is dedicated to our five wonderful grandchildren

Anna, Sophie, Kate, Rory and Emma

Chapter 1

My Early Years

Nineteen-thirty-nine was the year Adolph Hitler invaded Poland and precipitated a world war of unimaginable horror and destruction, a war whose legacy is still with us today and will continue to be with us for decades to come. This was also the year that I was born to Kitty Redmond and Michael McEvoy.

My parents, Kitty and Michael McEvoy.

I am the eldest of four children, my brother Larry arrived less than two years later and my two sisters, Margery and Helen, sometime after that. We lived in one of the famous Kenny-built houses at number 51 Sycamore Road in Mount Merrion, South County Dublin. This neighbourhood is regarded as quite posh these days and even in the 1940s it had a certain cachet. Our house was a semi-detached, two-storey, four-bedroomed one which my parents rented from a Mrs Mulcahy. My memory is of interminable rows with Mrs Mulcahy. She was unhappy with the rental arrangements and keen to get the property back for herself. It was very difficult to get rid of a sitting tenant in those times and although the matter eventually did come to the courts, victory was with the McEvoys.

I have vivid memories of my parents, particularly my father who was a remarkable man. He was small in stature but incredibly strong, a gifted athlete, with a very high IQ, indeed he had a freakish numeracy. In sporting endeavours he was a natural at everything he attempted, including tennis, squash and golf. There is a story told about him that when he was working as a junior bank clerk in the Edenderry branch of the Hibernian Bank he won the Captain's Prize at the local golf club. Nothing strange here but apparently the next morning, after a lengthy celebratory night, he was on the first tee (a par 3) with his pals when he jocularly nominated a hole in one and proceeded to do just that! On another occasion he was chosen by his home club, Foxrock, to play in a special exhibition match partnering Patrick Campbell, the famous Quidnunc columnist with *The Irish Times,* against J. Lindsay 'Bonzo' Crabbe and Herbert McAuley. Patrick Campbell wrote up the story of the game in his Irish Times column, *'Paying warm tribute to my playing partner, Michael McEvoy, a very useful three handicapper'.*

My father's numerical skills were extraordinary. One of his party tricks was to scan a series of numbers in thousands of pounds, shillings and pence and write down the correct addition at the bottom of the page. Not surprisingly, he played bridge at inter-provincial level. I still recall being in the upstairs bedroom trying to sleep through his weekly bridge game with his partners including Tom Murray, Chairman of the ESB, and Kevin Fowler, the Comptroller and Auditor General when he was constantly upbraiding the others for their slow play, *'Hurry up, Tom, for God's sake, hurry up'*! He was also gifted with his hands and as a hobby used to make beautiful tallboys, coffee-lyre tables and such in our garden shed together with Bertie Hynes, a Hibernian Bank colleague. Bertie and I were to work together in the Ballymote branch in years to come.

Although my father prospered quite well in his later career, becoming manager of the Hibernian Bank's second-largest branch and then joining the elite inspection staff, he was a lifetime under-achiever. He had too much respect for authority, was always a company man and, I think, ultimately unfulfilled. In his later years he took heavily to drink. Yet when his alcoholism seemed out of control he gave up drinking overnight with the iron will which was one of his hallmarks.

It is a sad recollection for me that I never had his support and encouragement in my career; in fact, he actively discouraged me from being ambitious and always advised me to *'Play it safe'*. A particularly painful memory for me was his attempt to discourage me from entering University College Dublin as a night student to earn a third-level degree and shortly after Keyna and I were married, he declined to sign a guarantee to help us buy a house. And yet, I miss him deeply and in spite of all this I wish he was alive now so that I could help him, put my arms around him and encourage him to achieve his potential. He was a very male man, full of honesty and full of courage; I only wish that I could also remember him as a loving father but I suppose that's the way parents were in those days.

As in many families of the day there were victorian values and influences in our household during my youth. Strong moral values were to the fore as was the leading of an upstanding life and a sense of responsibility towards others. The victorian notion of male superiority and a supportive wife was dominant. In an early memory that I have of my father I put him as being in control in the house but well short of dominion. He was the authority symbol for me and my siblings. On looking back, I feel that my parents had great difficulty in expressing their love for us children. On my father's side, I think that he felt there was something unmanly about overt expressions of affection and I'm sure in this he was like many men of his generation.

My mother and father were totally devoted to each other. If my father was the archetypal male, my mother was the epitome of a certain type of female. She was quiet and self-effacing, relying on her husband for everything. It never occurred to my father that she might need to become more self-sufficient. With sad consequences, after he died, she was ill-equipped to deal with practical day-to-day matters. Mother came from a large North Dublin family and throughout her life she remained in awe of her mother, repeatedly using Grandmother Redmond as the example for how things should be done. Looking back, I think that her personal growth was stunted by this inability to break free of her mother's influence.

Occasionally, however, a different woman emerged and it brings home to me what she might have become. A good example was when she decided that I was to be educated at Belvedere College by the Jesuits. As a south-sider it would have been normal for my parents to have sent me to Blackrock College but my mother was adamant that it had to be Belvedere College, and I don't think my father had any say in the matter. Mother went to see the Rector, Fr. Kennedy SJ., and informed him that since all her brothers had gone to Belvedere College she wished for me also to be schooled by the Jesuits. She then explained that she could not afford to pay the school fees and requested that these might be subvented by Belvedere College. I do not know what the level of subvention was but I believe it was generous and that effectively I was a scholarship boy. This is ironic, given that Belvedere College today is famous for its scholarship scheme which provides free education for up to 10 per cent of the school enrolment for boys from the less well-off parts of North Dublin, who could not otherwise afford the fees. I am greatly indebted to my mother for sending me to Belvedere College.

Its effect on me was transformative, if gradual, and what I was able to do for Belvedere College in later life is only a small compensation for the values learned at this great school.

My father never trusted my mother with money and I have a sad memory of the time she mislaid a £1 note and turned the house upside down in a panic to find it. On the very rare occasion when she had a problem with my father she would confide in me as the eldest; she did not want me to take sides, she simply wanted me to understand her anguish. I remember the time that my father had a serious attack of the DTs because of his heavy drinking and we all stood around his bed, with my mother beseeching me to do something, anything. She had great and enviable faith in God and this sustained her until her dying day. On her deathbed her dying words to me were, *'Where's Michael'*? I remember replying, *'He is in heaven, mother, and waiting for you'*.

My brother Larry and I were very close in our youth but we jousted at times, as do most siblings. One afternoon while playing together I earned the title *'Carmello Man'* in circumstances which I can recall with a modicum of pride. My father had at that time a junior position in the Hibernian Bank and our family was not very well-off, so pocket money for the family was meagre. On this particular day however we had between us the sum of 3d. The issue was what we should spend it on and a considerable amount of time was spent surveying the windows of the local sweet shops. I was absolutely sure of my decision; it had to be one of Cadbury's renowned Carmello Bars. Larry was not at all convinced and he had a variety of alternative preferences. And so I set about persuading him. I went to extraordinary lengths to describe to him the delightful tastes that would be involved in swallowing even one square of a Carmello Bar. I commented on the alternative possible purchases, pointing out their limitations in considerable detail. I assured him that this was an experience which I had had in the past and that he could totally trust me that he would not be disappointed.

With my brother, Larry on the left.
('Sibling rivalry how are you').

From the standpoint of salesmanship I think I covered all the bases, extolling the virtues of the product, rubbishing the competition, and emphasising the reliability of the promoter.

Eventually he relented and gave me his 2d to add to my 1d and bring the luscious chocolate bar into the range of being a purchasable proposition. I was not disappointed but he was; sad to say he did not like the chocolate bar and after his first tentative taste declared he would have no more of it. I was not at all unhappy with this outcome; and in the fullness of time harmonious relations with my brother were resumed. It did, however, become part of family folklore and the moniker stuck. Very recently, for my 75th birthday present Larry gave me a lovely pewter mug; it was appropriately inscribed '*Carmello Man*'.

From our early years table tennis was a big thing with us. We played on the dining-room table which was well short of regulation requirements, even with the extra leaves in. In time, my father, Larry and I became quite adroit at this new form of the game. One day our father informed us that his cousin from Australia would be making a visit and he told us that this cousin was an elite athlete, having once played tennis against the famous Wimbledon champion, Lew Hoad. We could not wait to meet him. When he eventually arrived we greeted him at the doorstep and immediately ushered him into the dining room, placed a table tennis bat in his hand and asked him to show us 'his stuff' or something like that. With the advantage of the local pitch and the family as an audience both of us vanquished him, not once but twice. He was crestfallen and proceeded to complain about the table not being regulation size. Family legend says that I replied, '*But sure, it's the same for all of us, isn't it*'?

We had no television in those days but were hugely inventive in the way we used our time. We wrote stories and plays, we prepared our own 'newspapers' for sale complete with letters and crosswords. We also held raffles and we put on magic shows; but the really big deal was when we put on plays in our back garden, to be attended on a fee-paying basis by family, neighbours and friends. The plays were always full of high drama and grisly death scenes. It fell to me to 'author' the script and I normally ended up with the leading part. I remember particularly *The Prisoner in the Tower*, *The Wild Boy*, and especially *The Count of Monte Cristo*. In the latter production I was killed off in a particularly gruesome way, being poisoned by a cream bun laced with hemlock. I was required to die in the most horrific manner, with much flapping about and shouts of agony. When I finally succumbed the cream bun fell away from me and the play continued with me lying prostrate and motionless on the grass. After a minute or two of being out of the action my mind went off the rest of the play and back to the cream bun which was quite delicious. I then worked my way towards the bun, reached out and proceeded to finish eating it, much to the amusement of those who had paid to see our show.

Annual holidays in Ardamine, Co. Wexford were a feature when I was a boy. This beautiful coastal area with its pristine white sandy beaches is etched in my memory, particularly during my early teenage years.

Beautiful Ardamine in 1955. Guests and locals outside
the Weafer's farmhouse. My father is on the extreme right.

For a glorious two weeks in late July or early August we took lodgings in a farmhouse owned by a local family, the Weafers. I'm sure we had our share of rain but I can only remember sunshine, swimming, cricket on the grassy area behind the beach, meals in the farmhouse, coastal walks into places like Ballymoney and Courtown, and beginning to be aware that girls existed. Although my father was an outstanding athlete he could not swim and this was a source of keen embarrassment for him. I remember he used to get me out of bed very early in the morning before anyone else was up and about. We would walk down the beach, as far away from our lodgings as possible and, when he was certain nobody was around, he would strip to his swimming trunks and walk out into the sea to chest high depth and stand, just stand there! This for him was swimming. He would boast about his early-morning swim and I suppose I should be flattered that he let me in on the guilty secret.

I have clear memories of the meals in the farmhouse. We were joined by other families holidaying in adjacent accommodation and I remember that my father regularly dominated the conversation. Children were supposed to listen, not talk. I have a vivid memory of an occasion when I took a contrary view to the adult conversation and expressed a firm opinion on the matter. This was not well received and I was corrected by my elders. I recall saying something along the lines of, '*The proof of the pudding will be in the eating*'. This was regarded as impertinence of a high order and I was severely admonished, and embarrassed. I know my parents were a bit ashamed of me at the time but looking back I can understand. How things have changed! Keyna and I were significantly more tolerant of our two sons, Redmond and Dermot, when they were growing up and we always encouraged them to be themselves and to speak up for themselves. They are even more child-centred; they devote so much of their lives to encouraging the development of their children's talents and confidence. Their weekends and free time are taken over by the children, ferrying them to rugby, drama lessons, swimming practice, cricket matches, hockey and the like.

Gangs were also a big thing in my childhood. We were the Mount Merrion gang and we had leadership structures and secret

11

passwords and oaths of fealty and rules and punishments for infractions, the lot. We never really had a fight but felt that if we were called on to defend our homeland we could be relied upon. There was another gang called the Blackrock gang, these were a rough bunch of fellows and we felt they were of a lower status and of a lesser militaristic standing than we were. Mount Merrion in those days was Sycamore Road, Trees Road, The Rise and a number of other leafy streets, and behind all of that were fields and hills and territory for practicing manoeuvres. Sadly, one day we were attacked in a very cowardly manner from behind by the Blackrock gang. We were routed in total disarray, most of us running back to the safe haven of home. I was captured by the Blackrock gang and taken as a prisoner of war to the Blackrock stronghold. I do not know what sort of radio programmes these fellows had been listening to, or what comics they had been reading, but they threatened me with a pretty horrible fate and I was terrified. Eventually one of their mothers intervened on my behalf and having had my secret passwords stolen, and my pride seriously dented, I was sent back to the pastures of Mount Merrion.

I remember my pals from those days, Donal and Felim and Dick and Alan and many others. We were quite a happy crew who shared our comics when we could afford them and followed the escapades of Dick Barton who was a special hero to us. *Dick Barton, Special Agent* was a nightly radio show lasting only 15 minutes but in that short space of time the three heroes, Dick Barton, and his accomplices Snowy and Jock, inevitably managed to get themselves into the most horrible life-threatening situations only to miraculously escape at the start of the next episode. We used to go to the Regent Cinema at Blackrock to see early science-fiction films about the exploits of Buck Rogers, where we could gain admission for the price of four jam jars. The cinema was somewhat unhygienic to the extent that local people used to say about it, '*You could go in a cripple and come out walking*'!

Class at St Teresa's National School, Mount Merrion in the early 1940s (I am in the front row, third from the right).

We all attended Saint Teresa's national school from the age of four years onwards. National schools were very highly regarded in those days and Saint Teresa's, run by the legendary Mrs Moran was supposed to be one of the best. There was a big lawn in front of Saint Teresa's church and the national school which was originally part of the demesne of Lady Beatrice Pembroke and her husband Sir

Neville Wilkinson, the commissioner of the famous *Titania's Palace*. In my early youth it was the setting for all sorts of entertainment, including Fossetts Circus, equestrian shows, fêtes and carnivals. The 'big boys' used to play football there and occasionally youngsters like us from Saint Teresa's national school were invited to join in. I remember one such occasion; a soccer match was in its final minutes, with the score at nil all, when a free kick was awarded to the opposing team just outside the penalty box. The 'big boys' instructed me and a few of my friends from Saint Teresa's to line up on the goal line while the free kick was taken. The great takers of cannon-ball free kicks included Sir Bobby Charlton, the legendary Irish amateur athlete Dr. Kevin O'Flanagan and whoever it was that took that free kick. The ball was struck with incredible venom and hit me smack in the face. I recollect that I was credited with having saved the goal but that no amount of congratulations and praise could compensate for my pain and tears.

There were several quarries throughout the woods and one particularly deep one used to test our courage. The idea was that you got on your bike and freewheeled down the very steep incline, pedalled furiously along the bottom and hoped that you had enough momentum to reach the top on the other side. If you as much as touched the brake you would not have enough speed to complete the journey and were guaranteed to fall back painfully into the gully. We all took the test with varying results.

There were a few small shops at the bottom of The Rise, and there, together with my brother Larry, Donal Murray, subsequently

Bishop of Limerick, and the McCaffrey boys, I discovered the entrance to an ancient tunnel which reputedly led all the way through the woods and to the lawn beside the national school. We decided to explore it and for this purpose I borrowed my father's big silver coloured flashlight. I led the expedition and can still recall the mica on the walls of this tiny passageway and the water dripping to the ground as we gingerly made our way. As the passageway got narrower and narrower we were becoming increasingly frightened. Good sense eventually prevailed and with great difficulty we turned back and made it safely home. A few weeks later the tunnel collapsed in the middle of the woods and to this day the memory of the experience brings on feelings of claustrophobia whenever I am in an enclosed space.

Corporal punishment was administered for bad behaviour at Saint Teresa's but I don't recall it being too severe except when it involved stealing from the local orchard. There was, however, a certain rite of passage about stealing a few apples and most of us felt the need to prove ourselves in this way. In the winter, snowball fights were a big feature and I remember an occasion when things got out of hand. The infamous Blackrock gang launched a snowball war on the boys at Saint Teresa's, which was great fun until we discovered they were putting stones in the snowballs. We all beat a hasty retreat indoors with the exception of Rory Mulligan (now Fr. Rory SM) who continued to brave the assault and return the fire on his own.

I have one sad memory of a classroom experience when I was about eight years of age. The teacher had left the class alone for a short period of time when one of the girls picked up a crucifix and danced around the room with it, to applause from her classmates. In the middle of this rowdy behaviour the teacher returned. She quietened the class, put the crucifix back in its place, lit a candle and proceeded to burn the hand of the child as a punishment. It is a horrible memory that I cannot shake off, even to this very day.

National schooldays were mostly happy days for me and equipped me sufficiently well to pass the entrance examination for Belvedere College. It is a justly famous school and the Jesuits are famous educators. Among its illustrious past pupils was James Joyce, now held in worldwide acclaim, but in those days he was *persona non grata* with the Jesuits because of his strident anti-Catholic views in his early and mid- life. The school is housed in Great Denmark Street almost since its beginnings in 1841 and the richness of its tradition derives from North Dublin. Getting to the school on a daily basis took two buses and three if I needed to go to the Cabra sports grounds, or else an arduous cycle run early in the morning. The youngest in my class, I was quite lazy during my time at Belvedere College, although always placed in the A class for the full range of subjects. The school at that time had a lamentable system of categorising students into classes which ranged from A to D.

The teaching staff was mostly Jesuit priests or scholastics and many of them were memorable men. The Prefect of Studies was Fr.

Rupert Coyle SJ; apart from his duties in teaching higher mathematics he was responsible for administering punishment. Any of the teachers who were dissatisfied with the performance of a student in relation to classwork or homework or whatever, could give the unfortunate a written note which had to be redeemed by Fr. Coyle. Redemption of the note meant queueing up outside his office, first listening to others being 'biffed' strenuously with a leather strap and then when your turn came presenting the note, when an appropriate number of 'biffs' would be administered. I did not have this experience too often and it did not do me any lasting harm. I was mindful that the founder of the Jesuits, St. Ignatius Loyola, was of the view that it was inappropriate for Jesuit priests to administer punishment; instead he felt the better course was to employ what he called a *'Corrector'*. It occurred to me to mention this to Fr. Coyle but good sense prevailed.

In a somewhat different category was the famous 'Bull' O'Callaghan SJ. He carried a leather strap hidden in his robes at all times and if you happened to be sent outside the door during class and he came by, you could anticipate the leather strap being put to vigorous use. He was a gifted mathematics teacher and a passionately committed coach of the College Junior Cup team, sadly without achieving any success during my time. I did not like him nor he me but I do remember one illuminating episode towards the end of my days at Belvedere College. The class subject was Euclid's geometrical theorems and he called me up to the front of the class with a view to my demonstrating one of the proofs.

Frankly, I did not have a clue. I told him so and when he asked why, I said that I had decided not to study it in favour of working on some alternative subject. There was a stunned silence in the class in anticipation of mayhem raining down on me. But I think he saw that I had reached my limit and was determined to stand up to him, so he backed off and told me to sit down.

Tadhg Ó Murchú, a charismatic teacher of Irish, was one of my favourites and he was also in charge of the Irish debating team, of which I was a member.

The great Terry Wogan acting the maggot
in class at Belvedere College.

He had a great sense of humour; on one occasion Terry Wogan, later of TV and radio fame, was called up to the front of the class to be given a punishment note addressed to the Prefect of Studies.

Wogan ran up the aisle, got down on his knees, threw his arms around the ankles of Mr. Ó Murchú and said, *'You're only an old bully and I'm going to tell my Mammy on you'*. Tadhg burst out laughing, tore up the note and sent Wogan back to his desk. In stylistic terms not too much changed for Terry in later life. Fr. Peader McSeamus taught us Greek and Greek history; he was known as *'The Creeper'* and was held in affection by all. He inculcated in many of us, me included, a lifelong interest in ancient Greek civilisation. The Jesuits were always exhorting us to find and develop our God-given talents and interests, be they in the arts, sports, life sciences, or whatever.

Fr. McSeamus was typical of the many fine Jesuits who were at Belvedere College in those times. They were always encouraging us to be conscious of our responsibility to society and our fellow man and there were countless opportunities for us to become involved in good works. These ranged from being a member of the Society of St Vincent de Paul, to assisting at the summer camp for what was then the Belvedere Newsboys' Club, to raising money for charitable causes on flag days, and much more. Although the value and worth of my years at Belvedere College only came to fruition slowly in later years, I have no doubt that my life philosophy was shaped there. I was not a conscientious student at school. Throughout my time at Belvedere College, I sat beside my close friend, Ron Skelly, a talented fellow and a very hard worker. He had one unusual skill: if I was called on by the teacher to translate a passage in French or

Latin or whatever, Ronnie, who had done his homework and had a perfect translation available, was able to speak in a voice which could only be heard by me, who had not done my homework and was unable to provide the translation without his help. Hence I had a good, if undeserved, reputation for translation at school.

One pleasant memory I have of schooldays is about the so-called Bishop's Exam. This was a comprehensive test of religious knowledge under the headings of the Gospels, Apologetics and Religious History; traditionally a cash prize was awarded to the best performing student. Now I had read none of the books on the required topics until the Friday before the Monday examination. On that Friday evening, I begged, borrowed or bought the necessary books and I worked flat out on them throughout the weekend. Come Monday, the examination was presided over by the gentle Fr. Ger Branigan SJ. I believe that I was one of the few in the room who was not cheating by way of surreptitiously opening the textbooks to 'cog' the answers. I felt I had all the answers but had the exam been on the following day I would have forgotten everything by then. In any event I secured first place at Belvedere College and third place in Leinster and was awarded the prize of a 10 shilling note by the Rector, Fr. McLoughlin SJ. Perhaps this was a harbinger of things to come.

The senior classes at the school were traditionally involved in the Flag Day collection in aid of the Belvedere Newsboys' Club. I have to be honest in saying the motivation in this endeavour was not wholly altruistic, valuable prizes by way of free passes to the Carlton Cinema were on offer, depending on the amount of money you raised. I was actually very good at this and my recollection is that I was in the top three collectors. One of my keys to success was to do the collecting in the wealthy sites such as outside Sunday Mass at Donnybrook Church. At that time, flags were not stuck on to the lapels of those who donated; rather they were pinned on and occasionally with unfortunate results when the pin was pressed beyond the material!

I was very fond of music, particularly jazz music and I could sing a little bit. This encouraged me to put my name forward as a candidate for the chorus of the famous Gilbert and Sullivan operas which the school used to put on. I auditioned with Fr. Branigan and when he heard my first attempts he said, *'Paddy this sounds very good, let's hear a little more'*. Unfortunately, the *'little more'* was a bit of a disaster and I ended up being a tuxedoed usher during the opera performances, much to the delight of my proud parents.

I secured a poor pass in the Leaving Certificate which was facilitated by an event during the Greek examination, something which could not happen today. When the papers were handed out, in a moment of madness, I opted for the honours paper hoping that the text on which we were to be questioned would be among the very few with which I was familiar. Sadly, this was not the case and the honours paper was wholly unintelligible to me. The exam superintendent was a distracted fellow who spent the whole time of the examination practising his fly fishing skills.

My last day at Belvedere College.

I summoned up the courage to ask him could I change to the pass paper, explaining that the honours paper was 'greek' to me. I think he liked my witticism and wonderfully he obliged and I secured a pass in the Greek exam.

During my early life, we, as a family, would regularly visit my maternal grandparents on the north side of the city of Dublin. I have very happy memories of them and of their house. Memories are indeed strange things and not always accurate. There is an element of colouring and refining of memory until it accords with an image which is probably somewhere between the reality and the ideal of reality. The house was on Iona Road, a short distance from Belvedere College and I often visited there after school. In memory the house seems a good deal bigger than I now know it to be.

My maternal grandparents with their family.
L-R: back row: My parents Kitty and Michael, Bee, Maureen,
Joe and Peg. Front row: Larry, Grandad, Grandma and John.

In particular, I have an image in my mind of a very large drawing room, with a piano and a mandolin. The house seemed to always be full of music and chat, both my grandmother and my Aunt Bee being amateur musical composers.

I recall bellows being used for starting the fire, and mangles and washing boards. The washing was done by a very stout lady, simply known as 'the washerwoman', who had 20 children; this was not that unusual for poor families in those days. I can vaguely remember rationing after the war, when tea, sugar and soap were particularly scarce. I remember the time my Uncle Joe brought a banana to the house, which he had purchased for something outrageous, like five shillings. This unique fruit was then cut up into small pieces and everybody in the house got a taste and proclaimed it to be well worth the money spent. I have the fondest memories of Uncle Joe, like his father, he too was very handsome and there was always a frisson of excitement when he was around.

I remember Grandma as a plump, happy and cultured person, who took a great interest in me when I was at Belvedere College. She was, however, a domineering presence as far as her family was concerned. I recall an occasion when she lost her temper with a couple of her then grown-up children. I don't remember the details but she terrified everyone in the house. She was one of the Bolger's from Ferns, Co. Wexford, a family with substantial commercial interests and well regarded in the town. When Grandma was young she went to finishing school in Switzerland and became proficient there in a number of European languages and presumably in the good manners expected from well-brought-up young ladies of the day. I can recall copies of the Reader's Digest in the house in German, French and Italian. I always looked forward to lengthy discussions with Grandma. She was a very intellectual person and our chats ranged over everything from films to physics, from philosophy to religion, from world affairs to ethical behaviour. I have no doubt that she kindled in me an interest in things intellectual and for this I remain grateful to her.

My grandfather, Lawrence Redmond, was a very handsome man; he was some years Grandma's senior and came from a humble background. He was a commercial traveller with Clerys, a large department store and his area of responsibility was to sell to the Religious Convents throughout the length and breadth of the country. In 1941, on the promptings of Eustace Shott of Craig Gardner, Clerys was bought out of receivership by Denis Guiney for £250,000. My grandfather was led to expect that when this took place he could expect a directorship but in the event none was offered, which was a great disappointment to him. He had, however, invested wisely in the stock market and amassed a sufficient fortune to provide for the family. My memory puts him in the kindly old gentleman category. He was immensely proud of his vegetable and fruit garden, to this day I have never experienced loganberries to compare.

My favourite aunt was Bee. She was a spinster who worked as secretary for Mr. Conroy, the chief executive of the Odeon Cinema group, at the group headquarters on O'Connell Street, Dublin. I remember my Aunt Bee as a very attractive woman with a great zest for life and a keen interest in the world around her. She would have made a great mother and it was a shame that she never married. On my way home from Belvedere College I used to visit her at her office in the Savoy Cinema in the knowledge that I would be given free passes to one of the group's cinemas for myself and whoever was with me. An unforgettable memory for me was when she arranged for Mr. Anderson, also of cinema fame, to come out to our house in Mount Merrion on one of my birthdays and to bring along one of the old-style film reels, a Hopalong Cassidy movie. This was an almost unheard of luxury in those days. One of the tricks 'Hoppy' performed was to toss a silver dollar high in the air, take out his six-shooter and drill a hole through the middle of it. The silver dollar fell to the ground right beside his feet, with a perfect hole in the centre of it! The laws of physics had been well and truly countermanded!

Fannie was the live-in help at Iona Road. She and I had a great relationship but our chats nearly always took place in the kitchen, which was her domain. When she came to the dining room she would never sit down, feeling it was not her place to do so. Fannie and Bee never got on and it is both sad and ironic that when both of my grandparents died and their house on Iona Road was sold, they had to spend their lives together in a small house in Monkstown.

There were two priests in the Redmond family, Uncle Larry and Uncle John. Uncle Larry was the elder of the two, with John and his twin sister Peg the youngest in the family. Uncle Larry was very sensitive about his status as a priest but I know that he had a reputation for being a very good priest and a very caring man. He did parish work throughout his life, never progressing beyond the status of a curate. He was well known for his caring work with older priests who might be troubled because of drink, depression or loneliness. In the East Wall parish of Dublin's inner city he founded a well-known boys' club which made a big contribution to the local community.

When Uncle Larry was moved as curate to the parish of Greenane in County Wicklow my father, my brother Larry, and I used to stay with him in the parish house as part of our summer holidays. These holidays in Greenane bring back very happy memories; I recollect the wilderness, fishing on bountiful river waters and hunting for rabbits in the woodland areas. On one occasion three young men from the East Wall Boys' Club came to visit; not surprisingly they were dressed in open neck shirts and sweaters and shorts, having travelled by bicycle. Probably because they had no change of attire they attended Mass on Sunday morning dressed the same way as when they arrived. When they came to receive Holy Communion Uncle Larry, who always sang during Holy Communion chastised them in front of all the parishioners for the manner of their dress. This is the sort of thing he would do but they forgave him.

The twins, Peg and John, were late arrivals in the Redmond family, being some seven years younger than their nearest sibling. Aunt Peg was a lovely self-confident young woman in those days; being the youngest in the family she was not too far away in age from me and we enjoyed each other's company. Peg's twin, my uncle John, became a Jesuit priest and taught at Jesuit schools including Belvedere College, Clongowes and Gonzaga College, where he taught both my sons. Unfortunately, he could not accept the radical reforms of the Church after the Second Vatican Council and had a crisis of faith. Keyna and I were well married at the time and used to visit him regularly but now he withdrew into himself. He wrote to tell us that while he appreciated our visits and enjoyed our company, he now wished us well but he did not want to see us again. He cut himself off from other family members at the same time. I used to make frequent enquiries from my Jesuit friends about his well-being. It transpired that he was very unhappy, suffered greatly from depression, and was difficult to live with.

When he died in his early 90s the Jesuit priest who was to deliver the homily at the requiem Mass called me and asked for my advice as to what he might say about Fr. John. I told him of my memories of John's earlier days when he was full of the joys of life, had outstanding acting and debating talents and was generally regarded as great company. My advice was acted on in the homily but in addition we were reminded that on the day of his death the Jesuits were celebrating the martyrdom of an 18th-century Scottish Jesuit saint who had died for his faith, the point was made that John also had died for his beliefs and his faith. All of the Redmond family cousins were present on the occasion of this requiem Mass. Over the years we had lost contact with each other but this event was to reignite our friendships and our sense of family. And so from the grave Uncle John, who had told many of us that he did not want to meet again, was responsible for bringing us all together.

Chapter 2

Early Banking Years
Part 1

When the war finally ended in 1945 our nation was in better condition than most other European countries; the policy of ambiguous neutrality had spared us direct involvement in the war and we emerged, briefly, with one of the highest incomes per capita in Europe. Other European countries enjoyed sustained economic growth throughout the 1950s but sadly Ireland did not, our economy growing by only 1 per cent a year throughout this decade. During the years when Éamon de Valera was Taoiseach and Fianna Fáil was in power, we were true to the aspirations and ideals of those who died for Ireland in the 1916 rebellion; the concern was to protect cultural values in the language, in our traditions, in songs and in the stories of the seanchaí. Artistic creativity was always high, with poets and writers continuing to produce outstanding work, yet many great artists left Ireland because of censorship and many ordinary people left due to the lack of opportunity. On the economic front the policy of protectionism was an unmitigated disaster and led to great poverty throughout the land.

Ordinary life had been seriously affected during the 1940s as a consequence of the war. People had to get used to widespread rationing of staples such as water, bread, tea and flour and there were regular shortages of fuel for cooking, for heating and for travel. It was 1949 before life began to return to normal and rationing gradually ceased. Commercial television had not arrived but the radio was widespread and popular. And these were very conservative times, particularly for women, who had to stop working outside the home when they married. In those days Ireland was primarily a rural society.

The 1950s were a decade of growth throughout Europe but not so in the case of Ireland where it is generally lamented as a lost decade. Economic progress was at a miserably low level and the newly appointed Secretary of the Department of Finance, T. K. Whitaker, was to pointedly ask whether after decades of self-government we could look to the future with any hope for economic progress. Indeed, 1956, the year I completed my Leaving Certificate at Belvedere College, was probably the low point, a draconian budget was needed in that year to deal with fundamental economic problems. And by 1958 the scourge of emigration reached its highest level since the foundation of the state, with the 1958 census figure recording the most dramatic fall in population since the beginning of the decade.

Having secured a pass in the Leaving Certificate it was decided that I should apply for a clerkship in the Hibernian Bank and I was enrolled in Rosses College to prepare for the entrance examination. My father had arranged that my sponsor for the Bank was Lord Courtown. I was still 17 years of age when I passed the Hibernian Bank examination and was excited at the prospect of the adventures that awaited me. At the time I had no particular ambition and little to offer: a pass Leaving Certificate, some good social skills, a clear understanding of the difference between right and wrong and a vague self-confidence based on a positive attitude to life. One of my abiding memories during my teenage years was discovering a book in my grandmother's house called *The Power of Positive Thinking* by Norman Vincent Peale. This book made a profound impression on me. I have always sought out the positives in my life and have always been a 'glass half-full' man.

My first posting in the Hibernian Bank was to the small town of Bailieborough in Co. Cavan where my title was *'Probationer Assistant Supernumerary'*. My parents gave me a fine new overcoat and £5, and sent me on my way. I was a city boy with no experience of small-town living and I was conscious that a big adventure lay ahead of me. The town is set in the hills of East Cavan and from the top of the highest local hill peak it is possible to see 14 counties on a fine day. I remember it as a one-street town with the imposing Catholic Church at one end and the local Catholic school located directly opposite. The Hibernian Bank, built in 1927, was at the other end of the town and directly opposite the Northern Bank.

The bank was a handsome enough building, but there any pretensions of grandeur ceased. The Hibernian Bank had no telephone and the only way to take telephone calls from Head Office was through the generosity of the Northern Bank across the road. There was an old-fashioned system for copying documents; they were first typed, then a blue cloth was dampened, the document to be copied was placed between the dampened cloth and a plain sheet of paper for the copy and all of this was inserted into a metal press. Serious force had to be exerted on the handle of the press, the plan being that a true copy of the document was procured and 'hung out to dry'.

The branch was known as a *'three-handed branch'*, although, given that the third person was supernumerary it is probably more accurate to describe it as a *'two-handed with prospects'* one. I was well received and it was noted favourably that my father was *'in the service'*. The Manager, Mr. Neary, was an avuncular type who soon started taking me for long walks after the bank was closed, with a view to teaching me the rudiments of banking as it applied to the taking of security and such matters. The number two, whose title was *'Teller etc.'*, was Mr. John F. McGee, an elderly, pleasant and somewhat ponderous individual. He spoke so slowly that I had the habit, not intending any rudeness, of finishing his sentences for him. Sadly, in our time together I never managed to end any sentence to his satisfaction. I have often reflected on this and have concluded that, even where my guess was correct, John F. McGee was determined not to give me this pleasure.

My role at the bank was that of a 'dogs-body', fetching and carrying, doing the copying, keeping the postage book and as time progressed graduating to the making of some ledger entries. I was absolutely without ambition at the time but intrigued with the novelty of my new situation. It seemed to me a pity that the tasks which I was given were ones to which I was not particularly well suited but I did my best. My initial salary was £190 per annum and, after heroic efforts, the Irish Bank Officials' Union, under the redoubtable leadership of Mr. John Titterington, secured an across-the-board increase for all banking staff throughout the country, which in my case meant an increase to £250 per annum.

My first lodgings or 'digs' as they were called were satisfactory in the sense that they were within short walking distance of the bank but in all other respects they were a bit of a hellhole. The landlady gave the impression of being constantly in fear of something, almost certainly related to the fact that she was married to a bully and a drunkard, she was so timorous when he was around. He was loud-mouthed and demanding. They had a little dog that was incredibly aggressive; the animal used to regularly meet me at the gate and attempt to chew my trouser leg off; I had to beat him away. The other positive feature was that my abode was very affordable, so I took the view that this was all part and parcel of the great new adventure. It did settle down a bit over time, principally because the landlord became more inclined to pass out from the drink rather than shout at his wife. I often wonder what became of them.

My social life was satisfactory; there was tennis, badminton, female company and house parties, and it seemed that even a probationer assistant supernumerary had some status in the town. In particular, I remember that John F. McGee and I, together with a gentleman named Ennis from the Northern Bank, used to go to the nearby town of Virginia to play doubles tennis on the lakeside shore of the Park Hotel. I can't remember how Mr. McGee travelled, but I went by way of the pillion on Ennis's motorbike and it was a miracle that he never had a crash while I was on board, he seemed to have regular crashes when he was on his own. I was disappointed to find that there was no table tennis club in Bailieborough but very pleased when I heard that such a facility was available in Virginia. So I set off on my bicycle and on arriving in Virginia went to the local town hall where, to my delight, table tennis matches were in progress. I asked about joining the club and in return I was asked where I came from. Explaining that I had come from Bailieborough, I was informed that the table tennis club was for local people only. I got on my bike, went back to Bailieborough and forgot about my plans for table tennis.

In 1957 the Irish retail banking scene comprised eight banks with stock market quotations, each of which had a network of branches throughout the country. There was little or no difference between these banks, either in terms of service offered or in their attitude to new business. However, the image of each bank was very different, and thus there tended to be a difference in the type of clientele with which they did business. The Bank of Ireland, the largest of the so-called joint stock banks, was seen as the most conservative bank in a highly conservative industry. The Bank was founded by English Royal Charter in the latter part of the 18th century. For a short time it had a monopoly of the note issue, and for decades enjoyed such perquisites as handling the government account. Its head office was located in what was formerly known as Ireland's 'Parliament House'. Their traditional clients were larger business firms and the upper middle class. They were viewed as being conservative, anglicised, Protestant and overly formal. Over time, they consolidated this image by recruiting staff largely from Protestant schools and by appearing to some to discriminate against Catholics in filling executive positions. My bank, the Hibernian Bank, was one of the smaller commercial banks. It was founded in 1825 by a group of Catholic businessmen in Dublin who felt that the Bank of Ireland was unfairly discriminating against Catholics. Its customers were largely from the professional sector and also smaller business firms and shops. The Hibernian Bank prided itself in having an intensely personal relationship with its customers.

There was a great deal of inflexibility about Irish banking. The so-called Irish Banks' Standing Committee, of which all the joint stock banks were members, fixed common interest rates and charges, and operated standardised working hours, thus there was no opportunity for competition between the banks in terms of hours of business and pricing. The banks all had the same recruiting policies, and rates of pay and working conditions were all exactly the same. Banks only recruited personnel between the ages of 17 and 22 years, and there was no mobility of labour between them and very little mobility between banking and any other industry. In effect, when a young man joined a particular bank he could expect to spend his whole working life with it. It was highly unusual for anybody making a career in banking to have a university or professional qualification. Indeed, prior to 1962, bank personnel were discouraged from attending university at night.

Competition for employment positions in banking was intense, with the job seen to offer security and status in the community and, though the initial remuneration was small, the long-run prospects could be viewed positively. Generally speaking, the young people who filled positions were from good pre-university schools, were from middle-class homes, had achieved average but not exceptional grades and had an ability to communicate well with people. The selection procedure was somewhat complicated by the existence of patronage, banks found it very hard to refuse applicants nominated by important clients. Until 1960 promotions took place on the basis of seniority; there was an assumed correlation between ability and years of service. If one learned the demands of the system, was an accurate clerk and had the right degree of patience, there was a reasonable chance of some day achieving branch managership, assuming one was male.

The Hibernian Bank had around 500 employees and about 60 branches with, on average, six staff at each branch. The Bank was run on strict authoritarian lines with, for example, letters to head office always being signed as *'Your obedient servant'*. Head Office was based in Dublin and communicated with each branch each day. The branch managers had absolute power to do everything except make loans or spend money! Head office vetted all loans in excess of very small amounts, and approval was required for even the minutest expenditure. Considerable pressure was put on branch managers not to have any bad debts at their branch and thus they were reluctant to recommend or make any loans which were not extremely well secured. Head Office maintained firm control both by getting a vast amount of documentation from branches and through the system of sending inspectors to branches approximately every two years. Branches never knew when an inspector was to arrive, but their arrival was something feared and dreaded by staff. Their function was not to help, but simply to find error, in particular, clerical error. They would proceed through each and every calculation on each and every page of each and every book and would document errors and endeavour to secure explanations from the officials responsible. They then made reports directly to the Board of Directors on each branch which they had visited.

A young man who joined the bank expected to do the dullest of clerical work for a considerable number of years; he expected not to be informed about what was happening at the manager level except by the most enlightened superiors. In fact, he was not expected to be able to act as a bank cashier until he had seven to ten years' experience, and he was not allowed to make expenditure decisions of even a single pound until he achieved the rank of assistant manager. Furthermore, he was subject to transfer to the most remote parts of the country at two weeks' notice and risked the displeasure of Head Office and jeopardising his promotion prospects if he in any way questioned these transfers.

All disputes were with the banks collectively, and the history of relations between the Union and the banks was characterised by bitterness and resentment. Between 1955 and 1965, there were two work strikes and a work to rule. The major issue inevitably was salary, and there was an underlying need to vent frustration against the system. In 1970 a devastating and prolonged strike and lockout was to occur, which was to contribute to profound changes in the Irish banking industry. At the request of the Government, the sociologist Michael P. Fogarty reported on this bank strike, on the factors that led to it and on the lessons to be learned. He was to list as predisposing factors the history of mistrust between the Bank Officials Association and the Irish Banks Standing Committee. And he was to highlight the exceptionally poor staff relations which prevailed for such a long time. Fogarty's vivid description of junior staff's difficulties, for example, the young clerk's attempts to get a clean shirt in a country town without launderettes and a disobliging landlady, had a special resonance for me.

The strikes were an agonisingly difficult experience for senior bank personnel. They viewed themselves as professional people and greatly valued their status in the community. The very notion of a labour action such as a strike was degrading and anathema to their value system. This is a point of view with which I was fully in accord. Even though so much of my early banking career was served in a junior capacity I always identified with the management side. Effectively all employees of the banks were part of the trade union, with a very small number of senior managers being exempted from a strike or lockout in times of industrial action. I was never faced with the prospect of responding to the union call to strike. Fortunately during the industrial actions of both 1968 and 1970 I was absent on study leave and exempted from participation.

It would have been a real moral dilemma for me had that not been the case.

The branch staffs of the Hibernian Bank were extremely resentful and suspicious of Head Office. Head Office was in fact made the scapegoat for everything that went wrong and indeed, the further away geographically was the branch from Head Office, the greater was the communications gap. Despite all this, bank officials had an extreme loyalty to 'their' bank, and this was acutely true of the Hibernian Bank; indeed, the greater the seniority, the greater the loyalty. Loyalty was neither to the directors nor to Head Office management, but to 'The Bank'. This loyalty was highly prized by those who came to have it; in fact, one was not allowed to claim it until a certain number of years had been spent within the Bank.

I had only been with the Hibernian Bank for three years when in 1959, the Bank of Ireland acquired all Hibernian's stock. Throughout the Hibernian Bank, the reaction was immediate and violent. Staff meetings were called and strike action was threatened unless assurances were given by the Bank of Ireland. Had a strike been called, it would have involved all bank officials throughout the country and not only Hibernian Bank staff. The fears were threefold: the prospect of redundancy due to rationalisation of branches; the fear that a head office which was disliked would be replaced by a head office which was unknown; and, crucially, the fear that identity would be lost, that the Catholic, Irish, personal image which the employees saw their bank to have would disappear. These fears of insecurity were partially allayed by the

Bank of Ireland giving guarantees that there would be no rationalisation of branches or lessening of promotion opportunities, there would be no loss of character or identity, and each bank would function autonomously and would maintain its head office and Board of Directors, as before. But the writing was on the wall. Loyalty was severely undermined, and increasingly worried senior officials expressed the view that the day of their retirement would not arrive soon enough. The Bank of Ireland came to be seen as a rival, and the many circulars suggesting ways the two banks might co-operate were largely ignored.

Three years after my sojourn in Bailieborough and after a couple of small detours, I was instructed to report for duty to the town of Ballymote in Co. Sligo. Ballymote was a market town, whose hinterland was much admired for its craggy beauty. In Ballymote Castle it had the last and the mightiest of the Norman castles in Connaught. In 1960 its population was a mere 1,145 people. My time there was to occasion a truly transformational event in my life.

I was the junior at the branch, the other staff being the manager, an accountant, and a senior bank official. Nobody could have prepared me for the life which was in store for me in the west of Ireland. There is a story told about the branch that, on one occasion, the inspectors arrived from Dublin and to their dismay found the front door open with no staff in attendance, ledgers open on the counter, and even the odd pound note floating around. This was the most appalling vista they had ever experienced and, after overcoming their initial shock, the more senior of the two inspectors suggested that a good strategy might be to press the burglar alarm to see what would happen. The story goes that nothing happened for a short time and then a smartly dressed waiter arrived from the hotel across the road bearing drinks on a tray! If this story is not true, it should be.

The branch was a very happy one, and the Branch Manager 'Ginger' Martin was a particularly outgoing person. The second in charge at the branch was Bertie Hynes; he was a good friend of my father and I had met him in our Mount Merrion home when I was a youngster. During my time in Ballymote I was to learn about the extent of poverty in the town, quite a few of the Bank's customers had long overdue debts. There was one old farmer who had what was known as a 'past due' bill and he always sought out Mr. Hynes when he came into the office to pay a few pounds off his account. Bertie always treated him with the greatest of courtesy and respect. One day he came in and paid the whole thing off with a great flourish, he had been the beneficiary of money from America. *'Mr. Hynes'* he said, *'you have been very good to me in the bad times, there will be a beast in it for you'*. So we all waited in keen anticipation of this four-legged gift. About a month later the old farmer arrived in again and presented Bertie with one of the scrawniest chickens I have ever seen.

My lodgings were attached to Michael Cregan's general store, where I shared a room with Des Kilkenny who was the senior bank official in the Bank. The town was full of great characters, most

41

notably a fellow called Paddy Mullen who was deputy head at the local post office.

Paddy Mullen's and Carmel Farry's engagement party – all the great characters are there.

Paddy was a perpetual motion machine, the most energetic and imaginative fellow I have ever met. He was a gifted athlete who played Gaelic football and hurling for the county, occasionally played soccer for Sligo Rovers, was a very fine tennis player and a natural organiser. I remember he would sometimes come into the office in the morning, hail the Manager and say something along the lines of, '*Ginger, I presume you don't mind if we take Paddy for the afternoon to play centre forward in the soccer match I have organised between the north and south of the town'? 'No problem, Paddy'* the Manager would reply.

I did not take a drink at that time, but I would often join the local lads for marathon drinking sessions at Farry's pub, Carmel Farry was Paddy's fiancée. The locals used to order their bottles of beer three at a time and drink until well after closing time. On one occasion, we were raided by an overly officious local Garda to the consternation of all concerned, mainly because the local District Justice was among the revellers. He was shunted out the bathroom window before the Garda gained entrance. Subsequently, all were prosecuted in front of the same District Justice and with an absolutely straight face he fined everybody £3.

Another preoccupation was table tennis, and this is something I was very much in favour of as I was quite a useful player. We did not have a decent hall for our matches but the locals knew that the parish hall would be an ideal venue. However, no one was willing to approach Archdeacon Roughneen to ask his permission for the use of the hall. The Archdeacon ruled the town with an iron fist. He would make pronouncements from the altar such as *'There will be no snow-balling in the streets'* and on one occasion when the local doctor sought to leave the church before the celebrant had reached the sacristy, the Archdeacon's man physically held up the doctor until permission was granted from the altar for him to leave.

The Archdeacon was a huge man who had spent many years in the United States and was rumoured to have been a sparring partner to the great Max Baer, a former heavyweight boxing champion of the world. The general feeling was that Baer was a brave man to get into the ring with Roughneen. He had a palatial house on the outskirts of the town, and his summer guests included luminaries such as President Seán T. O'Kelly, the two of them would sit out on the patio to be admired by gaping townsfolk. I was deputised to visit the Archdeacon and request that we might be allowed to use the parish hall for table tennis. This I did. I was made to spend a considerable amount of time in an ante-room and was eventually shown into a luxurious reception room. *'How much will you pay'*?, asked the Archdeacon. I offered him 10 shillings, this was agreed, and for all I know the parish hall is still used for table tennis.

There was an annual table tennis fixture in the parish hall of an outlying town called Glen against a University College Galway (UCG) table tennis team. On one occasion, they brought a really good team to play us; our team included Paddy Mullen, Jimmy O'Donnell, of Leitrim football fame and myself. I could never beat either of these two players but I was worth my place as number three. The UCG team duly won the match and Paddy Mullen decided that an individual tournament should now take place on a knockout basis. I played my best-ever table tennis and beat Jimmy O'Donnell in the semi-final and was now drawn against the number one player from the UCG team in the final. I will never forget it. Elite sportsmen talk about *'getting in the zone'*, well, I did, that night. Everything seemed to slow down and no matter how hard he hit the ball, I seemed to have ample time to return it with under-spin. The match seemed to go on forever but eventually reached one set all and 20 each in the decider. My opponent had been hitting smashes down the left and right-hand side and I was mostly returning them with sliced backhands and forehands. At last, he made an uncharacteristic mistake and I had match point. Another rally ensued, again punishing forehands from him and chopped spin-laden returns from me. And then he popped one up a little bit on my backhand and I leaned in and played a crosscourt smash apparently to my right but in fact disguised and going straight down the left-hand side of the table. I had won.

The boys picked me up on their shoulders and carried me around the hall as their champion. Orson Welles' biographer, Barbara Leaming recalled that Welles claimed that as a young man acting in the Gate Theatre in Dublin he *'got all the applause I ever wanted in my life'*. Not really true, but that's the way I felt then and the memory does linger on.

My time in Ballymote gave me a real insight into the death throes of small-town rural Ireland. I became aware of the scale of emigration; it seemed to me that at least one in every family and sometimes the whole family had emigrated, mainly to England but also to the United States and Canada. The poverty of so many of the small population was obvious. There was little spending power from paid employment and a huge reliance on emigrants' remittances. Agriculture, which was dying, was the only game in town and I have vivid memories of mart days when cattle were bought and sold, sometimes by 'tanglers' on the outskirts of the town, but mostly at auctions in the local mart. There would be large amounts of cash in those days, which would be brought into the bank for lodgement in filthy dung-stained bags, counting it was a penance. The large number of pubs in the town would be overflowing afterwards and there would be drinking, laughter, merriment and song.

Like so many other small towns in rural Ireland, Ballymote was well used to emigration in those days. I remember two instances in particular. The first was a young girl who had been well educated by the standards of the time and had procured a qualification in midwifery in Belfast. She was from a relatively well-off family and for her going to America, where she had a sponsor and family contacts, was a great adventure. The party which took place on the night before her leaving for Dublin, and thence to Cobh and onwards to Minneapolis had elements of sadness in her departure but the dominant theme was one of congratulations, best wishes and *'Come home soon'*.

The second emigration I particularly remember was a sad occasion, more like a wake. The young lady in question had only Primary Certificate education, her family was impoverished and they could no longer afford to keep her. She had no realistic prospect of employment locally or elsewhere in Ireland. Through friends and I think Archdeacon Roughneen she did have a contact address of an Irish family in Boston, who were to look out for her when she arrived. I think she was terrified at the prospect of leaving her family. The party before her departure was full of bonhomie and the drink flowed but pain and sadness dominated. Most young Irish people who emigrated at that time had very little formal education and probably faced a life of hardship overseas. The fortunate few who had valuable qualifications such as nursing were in the minority and they could look forward to employment opportunities wherever they went in the English-speaking world. For them it was an adventure at a young age in their life and while, in later years, they would probably suffer the pain of loss of family and friends, there were compensations. Emigration was to rear its head again in the 1980s but this time the young people forced to leave the country would be much better educated than their predecessors, with many having third level qualifications, a positive consequence of the government's introduction of free second level education and support for access to third level in the 1960s.

Despite the regular tragedy of family members emigrating, and despite the absence of wealth, Ballymote was a happy town. There was always a sense of fun and community and there were countless ways to pass the time. This sense of support for others is an abiding memory I have; I remember, for example, that when turf had to be cut I was given time off from the bank to join in the turf cutting. I remember when Paddy Mullen built his house in preparation for his marriage to Carmel Farry that he was given free assistance by friends for the plumbing, the electrical work, the painting, whatever it took. It was a type of barter system where Paddy in turn would have been among the first to help others when they needed it.

Ballymote was full of memorable characters. Gerry Cassidy ran a little corner grocery shop, which incidentally was the beneficiary of a rare occasion during my early banking years when the Hibernian Bank provided some funding for a new venture. From time to time

Gerry would leave his shop, and come out to the footpath where he held forth on whatever issues of the day were on his mind. He normally attracted a small crowd and my memory is that he could be both eloquent and witty in repartee. Along with so many other locals he had a cheerful approach to life and he and they were deservedly full of confidence when they were on their own patch. However, it was different when they left their milieu; for example, when we all went to Croke Park to see Jimmy O'Donnell, the junior at the local Ulster Bank, playing in the All-Ireland semi-final against Cavan they remained silent; awed perhaps. This lack of confidence in the city surroundings was such a great pity because they were so much more talented than their Dublin counterparts. At that time Jimmy O'Donnell was smitten with Gerry Cassidy's sister, Rosie but she chose the nunnery instead of him.

Berchmans Scully was a good friend of mine; he and I played rugby with the nearby Ballina team. When the Ballina team selectors heard that I had been educated at Belvedere College they assumed that I followed the Belvedere College rugby traditions and chose me for a match. I scored my finest and luckiest of tries on that occasion; the opposing team was well into our half when I took a quick throw-in and ran the length of the pitch to score under the post. Based on that, and together with Berchmans, an excellent scrum-half, I was chosen to represent a Ballina/Sligo team to play in an exhibition match against what was then a very famous Galwegians team; they had several internationals and Irish final trialists in their ranks at the time, including people like Dooley,

O'Sullivan, Guerin and McEvoy (no relation). The big match was on a Saturday and it clashed with an engagement which Scully and I had to play in a soccer match in Sligo town. We felt we could do both; so we played the soccer match in appalling weather conditions and then moved on to Galway. We arrived just in time for the big exhibition match to note that everyone else was wearing Persil-white shorts and we were in mud-splattered attire. The match was a bit of a disaster for me; I was severely challenged in the scrum, in the line-out and about the pitch generally but Berchmans and I still had plenty of energy left, so after the celebratory dinner we went to a disco where we stayed until 2a.m. and then drove back to Ballymote.

The Ursuline Sisters ran a prestigious Home Economics College for young ladies on the shores of beautiful Loch Gill. The maximum number allowed per class was 12 and over the years it had been their practice to place each of these students in an adjacent town for the purpose of some practical work experience. The lovely Keyna McDwyer was accordingly sent to Ballymote as part of her teacher training, and as fate would have it she stayed at Michael Cregan's guesthouse, my digs. I was immediately smitten by her. Sad to record, my room-mate Des Kilkenny and I tossed a coin to determine who would have the first option to date the beautiful Keyna. Happily my luck was in and I won the toss. My account of our first meeting is based on Keyna's recollections.

'The two of us were alone in the lounge and Paddy was busying himself with letter writing or something like that and occasionally

49

directing some comment to me. I told him that "I would prefer if he could make up his mind as to whether he wished to write his letters or have a conversation with me". The choice was his'.

I understand that I did put away my letters and said something along the lines of, *'If I was to ask you to come to the pictures with me, would you be interested'? 'I don't answer hypothetical questions',* was her reply.

So, apparently I reframed my question in an acceptable format and the next evening we went to the local cinema to see Joanne Woodward in *The Three Faces of Eve.* Thus began a courtship that would shortly lead to our falling in love and in due course devoting our lives to each other. After a relatively short stay in the town during which Keyna got some practical teaching experience at the local technical school she went back to St Angela's. We continued to see each other as often as we could, sometimes double dating with some of Keyna's student friends along with their boyfriends.

The regimen at Saint Angela's College was extremely strict, and generally it was very difficult for the girls to be allowed out for an unchaperoned date. One particular exception comes to mind. The Saint Angela's girls were given a special permission to attend a dance at the famous Strandhill Ballroom on the strict understanding that they would be back no later than 11.30 pm. Berchmans and I escorted Keyna and her good friend Eileen Nestor to the dance, where the famous Acker Bilk was providing the music. Berchmans family had a number of businesses in Ballymote, one of them being a taxi service so he provided 'the wheels' for the big night.

A chaperoned date with Keyna at St. Angela's College,
Lough Gill, County Sligo.

My memory is a bit hazy about what happened next, suffice it to say that we left the dance hall in plenty of time, when despite repeated efforts, Berchmans was unable to get the car started. By the time we knew that we would have to consider an alternative plan to get home, the dance hall was empty, everybody had gone home and there were no taxis or telephones available.

We walked all the way from Strandhill to Saint Angela's, a distance of about 12 miles. We left the girls at the entrance to the College at about 2.30 in the morning and beat a hasty retreat. Keyna subsequently informed me that the whole community of nuns and all of their students were holding a prayer vigil for the safe return of herself and Eileen. Berchmans and I then walked back into Sligo town, a distance of about five miles, and from there we set out on the final ten-mile walk back to Ballymote. At about six o'clock in the morning we hailed a passing ice-cream van, the driver and the passenger seat were occupied but the driver kindly offered to transport us if we would climb into the refrigeration unit of the van for the remainder of the journey home. I do not recommend this mode of transport. I arrived back in Ballymote nearly as frozen as an ice-cream cone and with just about enough time to freshen up in my room and thence straight to the bank, it being a Monday morning. I actually fell asleep at work that morning; apparently my pen had dug a hole in the ledger and the ink was spreading out in an ever-widening circle. Amazingly, there were no recriminations and I was sent home. As a postscript I should say that we sent a very contrite letter to the nuns at St Angela's and sent them a gift to the limit of our financial resources. Apparently this was very well received and, in consideration of all the facts, we were deemed to have behaved in a reasonably gentlemanly manner and were forgiven. There were, however, no more dances permitted for the remainder of Keyna's student days.

My next posting was for six months in Sligo town which suited me very well, mainly because I was able to keep up my courtship of Keyna. Sligo was a wonderful place to live and work in and the social life was extraordinarily diverse, primarily based around tennis and the local amateur dramatics group. I had achieved some success with the Ballymote Players, with lead roles in Lennox Robinson's *Drama at Inish* and Philip Johnson's *Master Dudley*, both of which we had taken to the All-Ireland amateur finals in Athlone, with distinctions achieved in the rural category.

With the Ballymote Players in Lennox Robinson's
'Drama at Inish'.

Drama in Sligo was an altogether different proposition; the group was of semi-professional standard and I thought myself lucky to procure a minor part in one of their productions.

In late 1963 I was instructed to transfer to the Ardee branch of the Hibernian Bank. On arrival at the branch I was met by the Manager, a Mr. McLoughlin, who quickly informed me, '*I hate official's sons*'. McLoughlin was a gnarly little man who seemed to be in a constant state of colic, and I was to learn soon enough that the extent of his hatred went beyond me. The senior bank official at the branch was a fine fellow called Michael Hughes, poor Mick, even more than me, was the catalyst for the outbursts of the senior management. Their standards were wholly associated with perfection in clerking, being defined as accuracy to the penny in keeping the ledgers, the cash or the post book, and secondly in having a script, for ledger entries, which could rival the penmanship in the Book of Kells. Unfortunately, neither I nor Mick had strong talents in either of these areas.

So I had a pretty miserable time; one episode in particular stands out. I had been seeing Keyna as often as possible on the weekends and this necessitated 'thumbing' lifts from whatever car, delivery van or truck was available. This was a surprisingly reliable mode of transport, and generally speaking people were more than willing to take a stranger on board. I took so many lifts in those days that I swore to myself that, when the time came that I had a car, I would be equally generous to those in need. Regrettably, nowadays I, like most people, have an understandable concern about picking up total strangers on the road.

It so happened that one weekend I had been to Sligo to spend time with Keyna. Although I was on the road at about 5 am, on my

Monday return the gods were not with me. Eventually I arrived back at the Ardee branch at 10.30 instead of the required time for staff of 9 am. The Manager and his assistant were both waiting for me and the Manager in particular was apoplectic. He absolutely refused to listen to my excuses and explanations and roared at me:

'McEvoy, I know your type, just because your father is a member of the management in the Hibernian Bank you think you can do what you want! Well, we will see about this. I propose to report you to Head Office and complain to your father'. All the while throughout this tantrum, he was kicking a satchel up and down the floor with considerable venom.

Despite the discomforts of the Ardee branch of the Hibernian Bank there were some moments of light relief. Shortly after the episode of my failure to arrive at the branch on time the Manager informed me that Head Office had ordered me to appear at the Kingscourt branch on the following Monday morning in order to 'provide relief assistance'. Normally the relief staff functioned from Head Office and their role was to provide temporary staff to branches to cater for holidays, illnesses and the like. However, on this occasion, probably because Kingscourt was such a short distance from Ardee, I was chosen for the assignment. I knew the branch was a so called *'two-handed-branch'* and therefore this would be my first opportunity to be a branch cashier. My friend, Mick Hughes gave me some tuition on keeping the cash and I left on the Saturday night to be sure of being on time on this occasion.

The Manager was one Frank O'Dowd, a country type, with a reputation for being quite a character. The branch was also his house and a little path led to the doors of both the branch and his residence. At 8:30 a.m. I arrived, bright eyed and bushy tailed, and rang the manager's doorbell. After a considerable silence the door was opened by a grumpy looking, unshaven individual, still in his pyjamas. He growled at me, '*Go away*' and closed the door in my face.

For the next 40 minutes or so I walked up and down the main street of the town, which is reputed to be one of the widest in Europe and coming up to 9:30 am I rang the bell, of the branch this time, knowing that the bank would have to open up shortly. I could hear the clicking of shoes on a tiled passageway and the door was opened to reveal a completely different apparition: an elderly gentleman with a roguish look on his face, dressed in a sporting type jacket and cavalry twills and wearing a carnation in his jacket buttonhole. '*Ah yes, McEvoy I presume*' he said, '*Good to see you. I think you'll find everything is satisfactory, shouldn't be any problem. Now, I'm off to the Naas races, here are the keys to everything*', handing me a big set of keys as he passed by. '*I've talked to all the customers and I don't think they'll be bothering you*' he said, as he walked out to the little wicket gate. Pausing there he turned around, '*Oh, by the way McEvoy, if Head Office calls use your discretion, there's a good chap*', and off he went.

I figured out the keys, after a fashion, and waited for business to commence. Nobody arrived for the whole day. That is, until ten minutes before closing time when a young fellow, who said he was from the butcher's shop across the road, asked me to change some notes into coins for him. He apologised for coming in, saying that Mr. O'Dowd had asked him to leave me alone for the day. I was able to handle this transaction and I complimented myself on my first day in a 'branch cash'!

The Manager returned from the Naas races shortly afterwards, beaming and a little flushed. He thanked me profusely for *'minding the shop'*, made me a cup of tea and then walked me to the bus stop where I got the evening bus back to Ardee. I assume that he signed and dispatched the daily Head Office letter reporting on activities; and that he locked up.

We had a visit from the Inspectors during my stay at the Ardee branch. The senior inspector was a good friend of my father's. He was not a very good friend of mine. He spent about half a day going through all the calculations in the post book and concluded that I was in error by one shilling and sixpence. I can still see his notation at the bottom of the post book in green ink, *'Unsatisfactory, one shilling and sixpence short'*. He also discovered a couple of corrected spellings in the handwritten ledgers that were used at the time, this type of thing was regarded as sacrilege. My father told me that when his colleague returned to Dublin he said to him, *'Michael, your son is a nice young man, but without talent and I do not see him going anywhere'*.

There were, however, many positive features about Ardee, including the beginning of my love for the game of golf, some rugby with the Dundalk rugby club which was headquartered at the Quinn's Ballymascanlon Hotel and friendship with Mick and Joan Hughes, who regularly invited Keyna to stay with them. In particular, I remember with great affection the four of us listening to Benny Goodman's music, repeatedly playing his famous Carnegie Hall concert, and playing Solo at their house until the early hours of the morning or more precisely, until Joan got fed up with the late hours.

My next transfer was to the bustling seaside town of Bray, County Wicklow. Bray was a very agreeable place to live and work, with a population in excess of 25,000 and commuter links between Bray and Dublin provided by rail, bus and the motorways. Known as the 'Gateway to Wicklow' it was one of the longest established seaside towns in the country. The town boasted a golf course, tennis club, world-class fishing, a sailing club and horse riding. As far as tourism is concerned, I was to discover that it was a time of enviable enterprise. For example, in order to encourage tourism they actually had a cable car from the famous promenade to Bray Head, which was set up in 1950 by Eamonn Quinn, the father of Feargal Quinn of supermarket fame, and this was to last until 1970. The difficulty of regular meetings with Keyna now became even more of a problem as she had qualified as a teacher of Domestic Science, and she moved into the world of teaching in towns such as Bailieborough, Bawnboy, and finally Belturbet, where her family lived. But we managed, after a fashion, with the help of many friends and relatives who ferried us all around the country so that we could meet up at weekends.

Keyna and I wrote regularly throughout our courtship and on re-reading the letters two things in particular stand out: the pain and loneliness of our enforced separation and also our lack of cash. Even small amounts of money like a few pounds loomed large in our thinking. So, inevitably, when the time came that we needed to save for our wedding, money, or more importantly the lack of it, caused us great distress. One of my letters to Keyna around this time captures our feelings so well: *'I wish we could get married right now darling, I am so unhappy because we can't. I don't know how the hell I'm going to be able to wait until September 12 months; I will be worn out with the pain of waiting for you by then. Every single atom of me is concentrated on you, darling'*.

Around this time the first stirrings of real ambition were welling up in me. One of my letters captures this well: *'Keyna, do you know that I only became ambitious about my career when I fell in love with you. It is something I realised this morning, I want to make you proud of me and I want to be successful so that I can make you happy'*.

This awakening of ambition for the first time in my life was a strange but pleasurable sensation. Looking back now, I realise that ambition is of very limited value unless the right environment exists for it to flourish, context is everything. The context of my world was now one of complete change in the economic and social world but also in the world of Irish banking. The 1950s had been a decade when emigration had posed serious questions for the prevailing philosophy based on an idealised and utopian rural life and the merits of self-sufficiency. The economic policies which had prevailed since the founding of the state were finally abandoned in the late 1950s in favour of selective free trade and the encouragement of foreign investment, incentivised with low taxation.

The ground had already been prepared to encourage multinational investment in Ireland when, in 1949 the Industrial Development Authority (IDA) was established, and Export Profits Tax-relief was introduced in 1956. The Irish economy grew at a rate of 4-6 per cent throughout the 1960s, one consequence being that jobs now opened for women. This was also an era of social change, with a huge improvement in access to health care, significant expansion in social spending and greater equality for women. In 1967 free secondary education was introduced and this was to have an immediate impact. It gave new confidence to the young and, at the same time enhanced Ireland's attractiveness to those multinational companies looking for an educated workforce.

Following on the Bank of Ireland's acquisition of the Hibernian Bank in 1959, the new group had retained the McKinsey consulting company to help them plan for a successful adaptation to this new Ireland and to find ways to overcome the Irish Bank Officials Association's effective bar on the recruitment of suitably qualified personnel. This was to open opportunities for me.

The Hibernian Bank in Bray town was both a happy place to work and a thriving business enterprise. Our clientele included prosperous local businesses, local professionals and a significant share of the banking business of wealthy ascendancy types. The Manager, Tom Lloyd, was a real gentleman as well as an astute banker, and he did everything possible to encourage my burgeoning ambition. On one occasion, he wrote to Head Office to suggest that I might be given a promotion, which was beyond my due but, as he said, *'Even if you don't get the job it won't do you any harm that I have proposed you for it'*.

The complement of branch staff was ten and my role was primarily that of acting cashier. The Manager was very keen on good customer relations and I can recall one occasion when a very elderly local farmer came into the Bank, Tom Lloyd spotted him and rushed down the aisle to bid him welcome. *'How are you, Seamus, you are a delight for sore eyes. It is fit and well you are looking. Tell me what age are you now'*?

Seamus happily admitted that he was 88 years of age to which the Manager replied, *'My God, I don't believe it. You don't look a day over 65'*. Much chuckling and some silence after which Tom Lloyd, in an effort to fill the void, said, *'And what age do you think I am'*? This was a big mistake. After a lot of scrutiny and cogitation the old fellow looked the Manager in the eye and said earnestly, *'I'd say you were about 90'*.

A big feature of my time in Bray was my involvement with the Bray amateur dramatic society. These were serious players and most of them were paid up members of Irish Equity, the professional acting union. I performed at a modest level, usually playing the part of a juvenile lead. The Ardmore Film Studios in Bray was a thriving enterprise at the time and very often they looked to the local amateur dramatic society to fill minor parts in film productions. In 1963, the film *Of Human Bondage*, based on Somerset Maugham's book, was being made with a cast including Laurence Harvey and the gorgeous Kim Novak. They needed an actor to play the part of an Irish truck driver with whom she would have a brief romantic dalliance and the local drama society nominated me for the part. I actually went as far as having a successful audition at the studios for this part. Imagine me and Kim Novak, well that's as far as it got, imagining. Firstly, there was the small matter that I was not a member of Equity, and more importantly the branch Manager, about whom I have said so many kind words, was adamant that time off for this sort of activity was out of the question.

Speaking of films, there was one little benefit to my job as acting cashier at the Hibernian Bank in Bray. It was our custom to accept the cash takings of the local Odeon cinema, this was a National Bank customer and they had no branch representation in the town. Mr. Fagan was the local Manager of the cinema, and he was so grateful for this facility that he offered me free admission to any film showing at the Odeon. There was only one snag; I was required to wait until ten minutes after the film started in order to ensure that he lost no paying customers; following this interlude I rapped on his door when, subject to availability, a free seat was provided for me. Thus, I have seen a very large number of films, absent the first ten minutes.

My early lodgings in Bray were at the boarding house of Miss Noelle Hennessy; I shared these digs with my Hibernian Bank friend and colleague, Pat White. The digs were comfortable and the landlady looked after us in a very agreeable manner. When Keyna and I became engaged to be married Pat White insisted that we repair to the Royal Hotel across the road from the bank for a celebratory drink. The problem was that this excellent hotel was also frequented by many of the Bank's customers, who, of course, knew us well. There was a procession of the Bank's customers arriving at the bar and insisting *'Paddy McEvoy's engagement was a huge event and needed to be celebrated appropriately'*. I was a novice drinker at the time and suffice it to say I can still feel the hangover!

I had by now done all of the things expected from a well-brought up young man, including going to Keyna's hometown in Belturbet to ask her father's permission for his daughter's hand in marriage and arranging for both sets of parents to meet socially. Both the McEvoys and the McDwyers advised against marriage at such a young age and in such impoverished circumstances, but there was never any possibility of their advice being accepted.

We were married in the local church in Belturbet on 27 January 1964. There were five priests on the altar, including my uncles, Larry and John and afterwards we dined elegantly in the Seven

Horseshoes Hotel. We then drove to Dublin in a little Mini car, festooned with bunting, and just about made our flight to London where we honeymooned at the Regent Hotel. I still remember Keyna's hat falling off as we walked across the tarmac before we boarded the plane, and I can see her racing after it, as it rolled along on its brim on the runway.

My salary was now the lordly sum of £600 per annum. Keyna, because of the marriage ban had to give up her job and was unable to apply for another. All our money went on rent, food and essentials; we were poor but happy. Our first home was on the Meath Road in Bray, sparse but highly satisfactory accommodation. From the beginning, our social life was full, mainly based around the County Wicklow Lawn Tennis Club. I had been a committee member of this famous club for some time and shortly after we were married it was decided to re-institute the South Eastern Tennis Championship of Ireland. In bygone days, this had been a very famous event on the Irish tennis calendar and luminaries of the sport were among its champions. The tournament was a great success although we had huge difficulties in getting the courts up to the standard minimally required for such a prestigious event. All the top names participated, including Joe Hackett and Geraldine Barniville, and in addition the Oxford University senior team graced the competition. The championship went on for a week and in the evening the bar was regularly frequented by former tennis stars from the past such as T.G. McVeigh, J.J. Fitzgibbon, Ivor Boden and many others.

Our wedding day on 27th of January 1964.

On reflection, I feel nothing but gratitude for the manner in which the players accepted the rather mediocre conditions we had on offer. But a great time was had by all.

In September 1964 I enrolled as a night student in the Commerce Faculty of University College Dublin (UCD). This was a joint decision with Keyna. We reasoned that our world was changing and that the bank managers of the future would need grounding in finance, economics, organisational behaviour and other areas of commerce. Tom Lloyd supported my ambition and aspiration, and he made sure that I was able to get the 5.30 pm bus from Bray to Dublin every Monday to Friday. After lectures, it was my habit to continue studying at the college library until the last bus left for Bray at 11.15 p.m. each evening. These were very difficult times for me, between trying to hold down a job during the day, the demands of the B.Comm programme and the difficulties entailed in the regular commute from Bray to Dublin. I recall a number of ways in which I used my time more efficiently; for example, I developed the practice of speaking large sections of lecture material into a big old-style dictaphone recorder and then playing it back repeatedly when getting dressed in the morning or during mealtimes. An even better ruse was to enlist Keyna's support. One example of this was when I had difficulty in understanding Professor Louden Ryan's views on collusive oligopolistic practices. Keyna, who was pregnant with our first son at the time, studied this exciting topic and then painstakingly explained the minutiae to me. I suspect she was at one time a world expert on collusive oligopoly!

Our first son, Redmond, was born on 17 November 1964, and I recall the many occasions when I would come back from UCD to find Keyna carrying a crying baby around the bedroom, this could go on until the early hours of the morning. On one such occasion we happened on an article by the famous Dr. Spock in which he described the phenomenon we were experiencing as, *'No more than a dose of children's colic'*, which he claimed should not be a matter of concern to either of the parents. We were not amused.

Chapter 3

Early Banking Years
Part 2

Meanwhile, banking in Ireland was moving on at a rapid pace; in particular, a number of important things happened in 1965, the year following our marriage. The Bank of Ireland took over the National Bank, the second largest joint stock bank and a bank which since 1960 had become very progressive and forward thinking. The National Bank had been founded by the famous Irish patriot, Daniel O'Connell, and was both Catholic and nationalist in outlook. An enlightened top management group, a senior member of which was my father's brother, Alphy in the National Bank had helped to develop excellent staff relations. However, an even more intense reaction occurred within the National Bank staff than had occurred earlier with the Hibernian, and again the Bank of Ireland sought to allay fears by giving guarantees that the unit banks in the group would retain their autonomy and identity, and that there would never be rationalisation of branches.

And then, McKinsey and Company, the international management consultants, who had been retained by Bank of Ireland, now submitted their report. This report sought to change the character of Irish banking: McKinsey proposed that a centralised management headquarters be set up, staffed by officials from each of the unit banks. Their function would be to determine Group objectives and to advise operational management of each of the unit banks as to how these objectives could best be achieved; the emphasis was now to be firmly on business development. At the request of the government, sociologist, Michael P Fogarty, in 1971 reported on the prevailing flat structures which were quite unsuitable when innovation and adaptation to change were needed. A great deal of new decision-making authority and responsibility was now to be decentralised to regional assistant general managers and to branch managers. Branches were now to be targeted for performance and a new emphasis was put on staff training and development. The concept of promotion by seniority was dispensed with as far as possible, and the relative importance of clerical accuracy declined considerably. In effect, new rules were specified which were anathema to the old system, and the ground rules for all had changed.

Interbank rivalry within the Group increased enormously. For the Hibernian or the National to take an account from the Bank of Ireland was a matter of pride. The Group Headquarters became the new scapegoat. Little or no effort was made at branch level to promote new services developed by Headquarters. The resentment and bitterness of the older men was intense, and they refused to accommodate themselves to the new notion of actively seeking business. Branch bank managers were uncooperative with Group Headquarters, and they jealously tried to hold onto the power and control they previously had. In many cases, the branches were faced with the dilemma of receiving circulars emanating from Group

Headquarters, to be told by their local Head Office management to disregard them. Many of the staff went sick due to the mental and physical pressures of the situation. Branch control reports were not used, they were laughed at as being useless, and many questioned the rationale of the planned change.

But profits and share prices soared and senior management took some remedial steps. Frequent lunches and meetings were held with staff, and better communications were developed with the Union. Favourable stock options were given to employees, rates of pay were improved at all levels and fringe benefits were greatly increased. Quite soon, another large banking group, Allied Irish Banks (AIB), was formed, in direct competition with the Bank of Ireland group. Every effort was made to replace in-group bank to bank hostilities with combined competition against the new rival. Staff training and development were greatly intensified, and management was encouraged to develop as high a level of collaboration and participation as possible among their subordinates.

The timing of my starting the night-time university course could not have been better. In search of enhanced profitability, the Bank of Ireland had a dilemma: the new aspirations required managerial executive leadership and the Irish Bank Officials Association was insisting that no graduates could be employed. The solution was to embark on an ambitious internal staff training programme, and employees were encouraged to apply for sponsorship for both university and overseas management training courses. I was in a prime position to apply, having successfully completed the first year B.Comm. in UCD The application form asked for development ideas on a range of possible topics such as resources growth, extension or enlargement of services offered and staff training. I submitted three multi-page documents proposing the establishment of an internal market research unit, formalised branch operations meetings, and setting up a student loan plan.

Initially, the applications were to be processed through the Head Office of the individual banks. I was summoned to Hibernian's Head Office by the Assistant General Manager, Michael (Micky) O'Dea, who informed me that my ideas were both impertinent and inappropriate, he asked that I withdraw them, and then they would put forward my application to the new Group Headquarters. I was further told that I was to be transferred from Bray to the Navan branch of the Bank in due course. I recall seeking my father's advice which, sadly, was to follow O'Dea's proposal and *'play it safe'*. I refused to do this and it transpired that the Hibernian Bank senior management was obliged to forward my application in its entirety to the new Group Headquarters. My world was to change forever after this. On 30 September 1965 J.J. (Jimmy) Fitzsimons, General Manager of the Hibernian Bank, wrote to advise me that, *'You have been awarded a scholarship to enable you to complete the course you are taking at University College, Dublin, and you will be released from your duties in accordance with the terms of the scheme'*. Being a full-time student at UCD was a wonderful experience for me. The last time I had been a student was at

71

Belvedere College when I was unfocused and less than fully committed. Not any more; now I had the benefit of being a mature student with a wife and one child and a second one on the way, and I desperately wanted to achieve the best possible degree result. The subject material ranged from economics to finance to statistics and to organisational behaviour. One of the less enjoyable lecturers was Professor James Meenan who happened also to be a director of the Bank of Ireland. His lectures took place in what is now the National Concert Hall at Earlsfort Terrace and were normally attended by more than 500 students. His subject was Irish economic history and his method of teaching was to read out from prepared notes. This material was a recitation of mind-numbing sequential statistics relating to agricultural and commercial growth in each of the four provinces of Ireland. His material came to an abrupt halt in the early 1940s.

I once had the temerity to suggest to him that there would be considerable interest among the students for a lecture on the emerging Eurodollar. Very reluctantly he agreed to do this, but on condition that it would be done on a Sunday morning and thus not interfere with the scheduled lecture programme. And so one Sunday morning Professor Meenan arrived at Earlsfort Terrace to deliver a specially prepared lecture on the new phenomenon of the Eurodollar and its prospects. To my great embarrassment, no more than 20 students turned up.

Generally, I had a high opinion of the teaching staff, particularly Des Hally (I had known Des as a fellow member of the Longford

Gardens Tennis Club back when we were both teenagers), and eminences such as Garret FitzGerald, former Taoiseach of Ireland and Professor Patrick Lynch. I made fast friends while at UCD, particularly with the members of our study group, including John McInerney, Dave Power, John Power and Barry O'Neill, all of whom had careers of distinction in later years.

During my time at UCD I was chosen as Managing Editor of the prestigious *Exchange* economics journal. I had contributed an article for the Trinity term 1966 edition on *Productivity Agreements—Some Implications* and in recognition of this, together with the other members of the editorial staff, I was invited to dinner at the Royal Irish Yacht Club by Professor James Meenan and the famous economist Professor George O'Brien. I can recall two things about that evening: no matter how hard we tried we could not get these eminent economists to discuss any aspect of Irish economic life after the 1940s, and it was also the day of the birth of Dermot, my second son and indeed the day on which Nelson's Pillar was blown up, 8 March 1966.

My record to date in exams had not been good, with only an average level pass in the Leaving Certificate, so the approach of the final exams in September 1967 was a very stressful time for me. But I had been work-shy and unfocused in those earlier schooldays and now I was studious and hard-working. However, I did not know where my intellectual level lay, what was the quality of the competition, or how would I perform on the day. And I felt huge pressure to justify my sponsorship from the Bank. Hard work does bring its rewards and one of the things I do remember is that my ability to concentrate improved enormously. I sensed the beginnings of a capacity to 'get in the zone' in the sense of concentrating on what was at hand to the exclusion of all else.

In the month preceding the final examinations, my close friend John McInerney came to live with us in Bray, the plan being that he and I would prep together for the finals. On most, but by no means all of the subjects, it was possible to review the questions which had come up in previous years and establish a likely list of possible questions for the upcoming exam. The next step was to prepare model answers, including what John referred to as a 'unique selling point' for each of these anticipated questions. We attempted to memorise these answers through the use of acronyms, a single letter acting as a reminder for a particular point to be elaborated on, this was the primary focus of our daily walks on the Bray Esplanade.

When the exams were over I suffered particular anxiety over one of the papers, statistics. Maths had never been my strongest point and the more I reviewed my performance in my mind the more I thought I had failed. I hate to say it but my normal positivity was well and truly vanquished at the time.

When I went back to the Bank I was posted to the Mullingar branch on a short-term assignment. One morning I took a telephone call from my friend Des Hally at UCD and Des told me that I had been placed first in the B.Comm examination and had been awarded First Class Honours. The branch Manager invited me to have a whiskey with him that evening and my joy was bordering on pain.

John McInerney had been placed second, so perhaps the daily walks on the Bray Esplanade had been a factor.

Having completed the degree course at UCD, I decided to sit for the final examinations of the Institute of Bankers in Ireland. There was prize money involved here and, given our relative poverty, that was my main objective. I took first place also in these examinations and was awarded the PC Bell Testimonial medal. This was a solid gold medal, which I had no hesitation in trading in for a bronze replica and £35. I was again invited up to the Head Office of the Hibernian Bank in College Green when Assistant General Manager, O'Donoghue, made it perfectly clear to me that in his view I had acted unfairly by entering these examinations with the benefit of a university degree, which of course hardly any of my contemporaries had.

I have long been an admirer of the great German writer, Hermann Hesse and my favourite book of his is *The Glass Bead Game*, which I have read and reread over the years. I love his wisdom and in particular that philosophy which holds that the correct path in life can't be mapped, and that the only good paths are the ones we make ourselves. Hesse has a wonderful poem in *The Glass Bead Game*, part of which reads:

> *'As every flower fades and as all youth*
> *Departs, so life at every stage,*
> *So every virtue, so our grasp of truth,*
> *Blooms in its day and may not last forever.*
> *Since life may summon us at every age*

Be ready heart, for parting, new endeavour,
Be ready bravely and without remorse
To find new light that old ties cannot give.
In all beginnings dwells a magic force
For guiding us and helping us to live'.

So here I was at a crossroads in my life, full of ambition and now with some useful tools and a piece of parchment saying that I had graduated with distinction from the Commerce Faculty in UCD. In the six months since graduating, I had been working at Group Headquarters as an assistant to the Director of Planning, a newly created position. There I discovered that I had a talent for creative product development. I had pioneered the concept of staff-saving machines which were to be prominently located in major commercial enterprises. They were designed to encourage workforce savings and to bring new accounts to the Bank of Ireland Group. Also, my colleague Louis O'Connell and I had introduced a new form of branch banking, namely a mobile caravan which brought the bank directly to the customer. This novel initiative was featured on Gay Byrne's *Late Late Show*, when the mobile bank was driven on to the stage by the famous singing group, *The Bachelors*.

By far the most important contribution I made at that time was the introduction and implementation of the Student Aid Programme. This was a labour of love for me, as it ticked so many boxes. I felt the scheme could be a real winner for the Bank of Ireland in terms of establishing an early banking relationship with young graduates, and importantly I saw this initiative as a real response to a community need. The one thing I worried about was sustainability. I knew it would be very important to get real involvement from the bank branch staff, and that the programme might need to be modified in the future in the light of the early experience. The genesis of this loan scheme was complicated, involving dialogue with a number of departments within the Group, including the branch banking structure but also the departments of administration, advertising and planning. Intense discussions took place with the universities and with the Union of Students in Ireland (USI). In due course agreement was reached with all parties. New bank branches were opened on the campuses of all the leading universities and a high-powered countrywide marketing plan was put in place. The *Irish Independent* gave it front-page coverage and also lauded the scheme in its editorial; photographic coverage was of Ian Morrison, the Group CEO, with Brian Lenihan the Minister for Education and Howard Kinlay, President of the USI. A student loan plan had been one of my development suggestions at the time of applying for the Bank's UCD scholarship so it gave me huge satisfaction to see it come to fruition.

Not least of my satisfactions was the attitude of the AIB. They were not pleased at the support and publicity given by the Department of Education to the Student Aid Programme. The Secretary of the Department sent me a copy of a letter received from AIB in which they complained, '*I wonder if you consider it quite fair that your Department should give the appearance of advocacy of a particular banking group"*?

One day in the early spring of 1968, I was summoned to the offices of the Director of Personnel to be told that the Group Executive wanted to send an employee of the Bank of Ireland Group on a two-year course of study at the famous Harvard Business School, leading to a Masters in Business Administration. Apparently an earlier attempt to satisfy Harvard's entry requirements had not been successful, but they were willing to try again. Essentially I was asked if I was interested in making an application to Harvard. If I were successful in gaining entry the Bank would sponsor the costs involved. This opened a completely new horizon, I was speechless.

The application process for Harvard was daunting, and the prospect of failure, with its implications for my future career, was a real concern for me. The bar for acceptance was very high in terms of academic qualifications, lifetime achievements and motivation. Even more challenging for me was the requirement to score beyond the 93rd percentile in the so-called Princeton Test, a measure of quantitative and verbal skills. I did everything possible to improve my skills through reading and practice, and gradually my test scores did improve. Statistically, a very small percentage of those applying to the Harvard Business School's MBA programme were accepted and this figure was even lower in the case of foreign students, where a strict quota applied. The centrepiece of the application was a 12 page detailed form, together with a myriad of appendices. I put my soul into this, polishing and re-polishing it like a jeweller with a fine diamond. I was not sure whether this bastion of capitalism would appreciate it but I put a particular emphasis on my motivation to make some contribution to the common good. And then I held my breath, for what seemed like an eternity.

Finally, the summer edition of the 1968 staff magazine of the Bank of Ireland Group *Bank Talk* was able to record:

'As we go to press word has reached us of confirmation of Paddy McEvoy's acceptance for the Harvard University Graduate School of Business Administration. This selection represents a personal triumph as well as an achievement for the Group, as the qualifications both in ability and academic attainment for his two years postgraduate courses are extremely high and probably without equal on this side of the Atlantic. In recent years some 500 applicants from around the world competed for 70 places for foreign graduates'.

A new world was about to open up for me.

Harvard scholarship for
Paddy McEvoy - Hibernian

From BANK TALK, the staff magazine
of the Bank of Ireland Group, Summer 1968.

Chapter 4

My Harvard Experience

Once I was accepted by Harvard I did expect to graduate but feared that I would be outshone by my American peers. I think many young Irish people in those days felt both intimidated and under-qualified when travelling abroad and confronted with the high confidence level shown by others, particularly in the United States. I know I did and I was wrong; at the end of the day I graduated with a Distinction Degree.

In my entry year Tony Athos was in charge of admissions. He had come to Harvard from Berkeley College in California, a campus noted for being at the forefront of protest and change and he set about putting together a class which would be notably more liberal than its predecessors. There was to be a greater emphasis on recruiting more blacks, Puerto Ricans, Mexican-Americans, and women, together with a greater willingness to accept unusual but high-calibre candidates who did not fit into any corporate image. The quotas for minority groups were still very small but it was the start of a process which was to gain momentum in later years.

Some critics claim that, *'Harvard selects men and women who are going to be winners and then takes all the credit later when they succeed'*. There is an element of truth in this. The quality of my classmates was astonishingly high. Many of those who had post-college experience came from the military, some had served in

Vietnam as Captains or Majors and others came from the Annapolis Naval Academy background having been officers on board nuclear submarines. Most of the younger men and women came from prestigious international institutions such as Oxford, Cambridge, Harvard, Yale, and similar world-ranking colleges throughout the United States and Europe. The class of 750 students, in ten separate sections, was predominantly male but did include a number of females and a small cohort of black students. The younger men and women who had come straight from their colleges were exceptionally bright; indeed a few of them were reputed to have scored at the 100th percentile in the aptitude test.

The Harvard years were among the most memorable in my life. It was very important for me to have family with me but the work pressures were to prove so demanding that the opportunity for time with family was limited. Keyna's recollections are interesting:

'Paddy's going to Harvard proved to be a great broadening experience for all the family. The Business School was quite family oriented and we embraced this life. There were courses specially designed for the wives and I particularly remember the brilliant psychologist, Professor Tony Athos. And there were parties at the end of the each week requiring a written analysis of casework (once a month). On the first such occasion Paddy wore a jacket and tie and I was also formally dressed, everyone else was casually attired. The next time we dressed casually and everybody was in formal wear (they were trying to do it our way); after that we all went informal. As we became acquainted with Paddy's classmates and

their spouses, they offered us help in settling in and in particular in finding appropriate schools and recreational facilities for the children. Paddy was gone for ten to twelve hours every day and when he was home he still had a great deal of study on hand, so I was very grateful for all this help in integrating and finding out how to live my life without putting pressure on him. I remember Boston and the Harvard Business School campus with great affection, so many of the friendships have endured'.

Ours was the entry class of 1968, a historic year in the United States; it was a privilege to be among the small group of overseas students admitted to Harvard Business School. President Lyndon Johnson had announced his resignation in the spring of that year, having been shaken by the Vietnamese Tet offensive, facing rebellion within the Democratic Party and besieged by anti-war protesters chanting: *'Hey, hey, LBJ, how many kids did you kill today'*?

Alongside the anti-war movement the struggle for black liberation and a reborn movement for women's liberation added to the upheavals of 1968. The campuses of United States colleges were riven with protest throughout the year, with black students frequently taking the lead. When four white students were killed at Kent State University and two black students at Jackson State, strikes and protests took place throughout U.S. campuses in what amounted to a general campus strike. Black students went on strike at the Harvard Business School in protest about these murders, charging 'psychological atrocities'. Anti-war actions grew in size in

1969 and 1970, with the most combustible events taking place following the May 1970 invasion of Cambodia.

I was conscious that the Irish banking industry was in turmoil, partly because of disastrous staff relations but also because of the winds of change associated with efforts to modernise the industry. In Cambridge, Massachusetts, I was allowed to distance myself from all of this upset. I felt the Harvard experience would help me find out more about myself, to identify my strengths and weaknesses and lead to a better understanding of my life philosophy and its implications. At the same time, I always saw the Harvard experience as a game; I always saw it as a place to experiment and did not worry too much about personal failures. I think if there was a grade for whoever got the most out of the School from the Class of 1970 I would have been a candidate for top honours.

I was very aware that Harvard was in the forefront of promoting the philosophy that the predominant role of business was to make profits. Business' contributions to society were to be expressed in terms of this wealth creation and the jobs that went with it and nothing else. I was not at all sure how all this squared with my view that business and business leaders had a responsibility to make a contribution to the common good. From the outset the work pressure was enormous; I normally left my house at about 8 am and returned at 11 p.m., Monday through Saturday. Formal business wear, suit and tie for men, was mandatory in class in those days. The long hours were all work time, including class time, intensive study group work, or personal work in the library. In the first year, we were all required to take seven courses covering all the basic management functions of production, marketing and finance, as well as courses in control techniques, managerial economics, organisational behaviour, and corporate planning.

Virtually everything was done through the case-study method. Normally, we were given three new cases every day, they could be up to 100 pages long and full of financial appendices. The faculty expected all students to be fully conversant with case material and, while students were encouraged to take the initiative in class discussion, they could also be called on without notice. The really smart younger men and women assimilated these cases from the beginning while the rest of us laboured but gradually we all got the hang of it. Class discussions were heated and raucous, and a good instructor could bring competing case 'solutions' to fever point, when he would walk away, leaving us to discern what we had learned from the discussion.

Throughout all this intensity I had the great advantage of my relative maturity. I was nearly thirty years old at that time and of course married with two children so I was one of the older students in the class and I had a certain amount of relevant business experience. Although we fought like hell in class, friendships were formed quickly and many lasted for a lifetime.

I particularly remember some of the people in my study group, like Bob Banta and Bill Allen; both of whom were brilliant engineers who helped me enormously in the quantitative area. And Mike Cavallon, a former college football star, who had amassed a considerable fortune while working in Southeast Asia, unfortunately he was prohibited from selling his stock for the two-year period at Harvard, a period when the value of his stock fell from great heights to zero! And there was Lance Funston, a Texan; sometimes he came to class late on Monday mornings and I could hear him muttering about being held up by his attendance at some board meeting in Dallas, and saying to Bob Banta *'Bob, what is this case about anyway'?* as he furiously thumbed the case material. As the case study progressed, Lance would become increasingly familiar with it and at the end he would sum up, brilliantly. Andrew Parsons, an Oxford man would poke fun at my 'Irishness'. He would, for example, put a potato on my desk to the amusement of some, including me. We were good friends and Keyna and I were to attend his wedding to Carol before we left for home.

An added pressure point was the written analysis of cases (WAC). The cases were given out once a month late on Thursday afternoon and the written-up analysis had to be returned no later than ten o'clock on Saturday night with a maximum word count of no more than 1500 words. The cases were unbelievably complex and usually required working through the night to complete the analysis. Our submissions were, rather oddly, graded by girls from Radcliffe College, which annoyed the hell out of us. Initially the best grades I could muster were in the pass range. This was infuriating, and in a fit of pique I greatly exceeded the word count in the next WAC, I was granted a High Pass Plus!

Mike Cavellon.

Lance Funston talking to Bob Banta.

Andrew Parsons.

One of the big features of the first year was the so-called 'Management Game'. In the class of 1970 there were ten sections of 75 each. Each section was required to elect three Class Presidents for the Game, and it then fell to the Presidents to recruit their team from among their classmates. I was elected as one of the class

Presidents. In those days we still did our calculations with slide rules described by one of my colleagues later as *'a piece of wood with logarithmic functions on it'*. The Game, however, was computer-based and was designed to incorporate a structured management approach to a set of business problems which covered finance, marketing and related topics. You did not learn a thing about any of these topics during the course of the Game, in reality it was an exercise in human relations. Each team made decisions for an invented company on production, product range and price, expenditure in several headings, R&D etc. A computer program collated each 'company's' decisions and produced results including data on overall ranking in profitability and stock prices.

It is difficult to describe just how aggressive a group of Harvard Business School students could be in such a situation. Apparently the Game had been successfully hacked in the previous year. So, one of my team members, Ned Goodhue, an exceptionally bright young man, proposed that he would *'break the computer program'* and ensure overall success for us. Ned could write computer software programs as if he was writing a letter. His proposal was considered within our team and it was agreed by majority decision to proceed with the plan. What we did not know was that the faculty staff, horrified by what had taken place in the previous year, had applied a patch to the program to ensure it could never be tampered with again. We ended up as second last on virtually every metric and, worse still, this trend was evident and unavoidable from almost the very beginning, when we had attempted to 'fix' the Game program. I was held accountable and blamed by my team-mates. Although they had voted for the attempt to 'fix' the program, they hated losing and they needed a scapegoat. I was it.

Our instructor in the area of Organisational Behaviour was Harry Levinson, who was on a visiting Ford Foundation Professorship. Harry, with his Levinson Institute, was a very well-regarded Freudian psychologist and consultant to industry. He realised that the high level of angst now prevailing in our class section was related to under-performance in the Management Game, so he invited my team-mates to critique my performance in front of the class. This they did with gusto. I particularly remember Michel De Carvalho, subsequently Chairman of Citi's private banking in Europe and married to the Heineken heiress, Charlene Heineken, saying: *'Beware of people who are full of talk but can do nothing'*. This presumably meant me. When my classmates had had full rein Harry invited me to respond. I had a decent innings and the outcome of it all was that the boil was well and truly lanced. I thought Harry Levinson was brilliant in the way he handled the issue, and I remembered the lesson for the rest of my working life.

For Saint Patrick's Day, I undertook to arrange a suitable celebration for the class of 1970. Among other things, this involved raising sponsorship and getting free drink from the beer companies and from Arthur Guinness & Co. We had to give a formal undertaking to the Guinness Company that we would not make the 'Black Stuff' green. In the course of this I met and became friends with Tom Flatley, a Bostonian who was born in Kiltimagh, Co.

89

Mayo, had emigrated to the United States without any formal education and, through hard work and talent became a billionaire. It would probably be more correct to say that Tom befriended me; he was proud that a young Irishman was at the Harvard Business School. Tom was a staunch supporter of the Democratic Party and of the Kennedys in particular. On one occasion when Ted Kennedy was running for the United States Senate, his mother, Rose attended a garden party at the Flatley's home in support of Ted's candidacy and Keyna made Irish Coffees for all.

Around that time I had the good fortune to meet with the famous economist Elliott Janeway. He was a prolific writer who had proposed the then controversial and thought-provoking theory that political pressures shape economic and market trends. He had influenced the policy-making of a succession of US governments throughout his life and now wrote columns with the *Chicago Tribune-New York Times* syndicate and in weekly financial newsletters, which he penned from his home. He invited me to his house, introduced me to his family and talked to me about his economic philosophy, a great privilege. It so happened that the Bank of Ireland Group CEO, Ian Morrison, was at that time attending the Advanced Management Program at Harvard. In the course of conversation I mentioned this to Janeway, who said he would like to interview him, which he did and he syndicated the interview in some hundreds of regional newspapers.

At the end of the first year we students were all required to undertake a summer assignment designed to put into practice what we had learned during the first year. I had formed a friendship with one of the associate professors, David Birch, who with others had developed a software package designed to optimise the selection of locations for new bank branches. He arranged for me to go to the First New Haven National Bank in New Haven, Connecticut, with a view to implementing and testing the software. My initial contact was with the Bank's Secretary and Vice-President, Paul Johnson, a warm and charismatic man, who was just a few years older than me. He and I hit it off immediately and he set out to ensure that my summer experience with the First New Haven National Bank was as rewarding and fulfilling as possible for me. Through Paul, I developed a close rapport with the Bank's President, Frank Chadwick a retired Admiral, and with others in the senior management group. I spent a considerable amount of time at the Yale University computer centre trying to solve technical problems with the branch locations software. It transpired that there was a deep fault in the program, which was eventually rectified through contact with Professor Birch back at Harvard.

Frank Chadwick invited me to attend management meetings of the Bank and encouraged me to participate. He asked me to assist in the preparation of the Bank's corporate plan, and he prevailed on me to conduct case-study classes with the Bank's management group. The Business School provided me with case material; including teaching notes and the sessions were attended by both senior and junior management, including on occasion the President. The exercise was considered a great success. After I left the First

New Haven Bank Paul Johnson wrote to Ian Morrison: *'In all the years that we have been hiring individuals for specialised summer assignments, we have never been as fortunate as we were when we hired Mr. McEvoy. He attacked his assignment with a determination and resourcefulness infrequently seen in an organisation that we rate as being highly progressive and imaginative. He assimilated into the organisation with uncommon ease and developed an understanding and confidence with all those with whom he came in contact. Most importantly, however, he produced a marketing study and outline plan of attack which I'm sure will be the target of projects of our organisation for many years to come'.*

A party was held for me on my leaving the Bank and I was presented with a small amount of bank stock, suitably framed and with the inscription, *'In emergency break glass'*. In due course the First New Haven National Bank was acquired by another and larger Connecticut-based bank, which was then acquired by New England Merchants Bank, to be acquired by State Street Bank in Boston, and finally by the Bank of America. And so, four times a year I get a small dividend from the Bank of America, it is a reminder of my debt to Paul Johnson for a great learning experience and a very happy summer.

By the start of the second year we had all found our sea legs and had become familiar with the course topics. Relations had also become more informal with faculty staff and friendships with classmates deepened. The work was still intense but somehow our capacity to manage it improved. There seemed to be more time for socialising and I have happy memories of picnics on the River Charles with Dick and Cathy Norman and with Murray and Barbara Nixon. I had fallen in love with America, with its style, its diversity and with its 'can-do' philosophy.

There was a huge interest in so-called T-group sessions at the time. These sessions were psychoanalytically based and designed to help people learn about themselves and about small group processes in general through their interactions with each other. A T-group meeting does not have an explicit agenda, structure or an express goal but the idea is that under the guidance of a facilitator the participants are encouraged to share emotional reactions that arise in response to their fellow participants' actions and statements. The famous psychoanalyst, Carl Rogers, called the T-group *'The most significant social invention of the century'*. Together with my friend and classmate, Danny Gallagher, Keyna and I attended one of these group therapy sessions at the local Tufts University. It was a disaster. The so-called facilitator of the group succeeded in getting one young man to open up about his inner self to the extent that with the encouragement of all he told the group that he was homosexual. He then proceeded to cry and shout, he could not be comforted. The trainer had been able to open this young man up but was totally unable to handle the situation that developed. Everything was unresolved and I can only hope that the unfortunate man was able to get proper professional assistance to help him deal with what must have been a very disturbing experience for him.

Football games at the Harvard Bowl were also a big thing and we once saw Harvard come from behind in the closing minutes to beat Yale in a very famous match. The Harvard Bowl also hosted memorable musical events including some of the great American classical orchestras and entertainers such as Janis Joplin and Ray Charles. The Janis Joplin concert was special. She arrived by helicopter, at least two hours late, clutching a bottle of Southern Comfort; she sang all her great numbers late into the night. The McEvoys and 30,000 others, everyone passing around marijuana; I cannot remember whether we indulged or not, if we did, like Bill Clinton, we did not inhale!

My grades following on the first-year assessment, exams, classwork, written analysis of cases, etc., were okay but unspectacular. My confidence was high at the start of the second year and I felt I could lengthen my stride. I had a special interest in organisational behaviour and had learned a great deal from Harry Levinson. His approach to our Organisational Behaviour classes was to demonstrate the practical day-to-day value of Freud's thinking in areas like the role of identification in learning, transference and projection of anger in company settings, and the importance of cultural influences in the development of conscience.

One of the features of the second year was the opportunity to audit some courses which would not be part of the final examination. Because of my interest in this area, I took the opportunity to attend Tony Athos' course on the role of interpersonal dynamics in organisational behaviour. Tony, who had in the previous year been featured on the cover of *Time* magazine as one of the United States' ten greatest teachers, was a very charismatic man whose course material dipped regularly into the areas of sociology and philosophy. Freedom was a big buzzword in those days and Tony used to talk about it a lot. He would challenge the class with: '*Freedom, yes, but freedom to do what*'? He was a hugely positive and optimistic person but I recall that his principle mantra was that there are three great certainties in life: uncertainty, ambiguity, and imperfection.

The second year was also different in that there were more than a hundred course offerings and seminars through eleven subject areas; we were required to choose five in addition to the compulsory Business Policy course. I chose institutional investment/investment banking/policy and strategy of financial institutions/marketing research and information systems, and my dissertation was a case study in Organisational Diagnosis. This was a study on the Harvard University Press, under the guidance of Harry Levinson. There were four of us in the study group, and Harry subsequently wrote a book based on our work, entitled *Organisational Diagnosis*. I still have a copy of his book, with the inscription on the flyleaf '*To Paddy and Keyna with esteem and affection, Harry Levinson—12/12/71*'.

I was elected as President of the Marketing Club, and throughout the year we had as guest speakers CEOs from some of the top U.S companies such as General Foods, MGM and General Motors.

The Marketing Club Committee at the Harvard Business School with Paddy McEvoy, second from right.

The best attended and most dynamic presentation came from the famous former Indianapolis 500 winner, Andy Granatelli, then President and owner of STP Corporation. *Time* magazine covered the event. My classmate and friend Bill Allen drove him back to Logan airport in Bill's red Mustang car and I accompanied them.

The famous Indy 500 driver, Andy Granatelli speaking to the
Harvard Marketing Club. He started his address
'I don't want to brag but it is difficult not to'.

At one stage Granatelli said to him *'Don't you think you're going a bit fast in this old jalopy'? 'Not at all'* replied Bill, *'I can handle this car very well and if there is any trouble I will know what to do'. 'Listen, son,'* said the former winner of the Indy 500, *'if this car gets into any trouble on the way to the airport there is only one person on board who will know what to do and that is me'.*

Bill slowed down after that.

Graduates of the Harvard Business School were the best paid in the United States, particularly those who joined the top consulting and investment banking firms on Wall Street. Many of the top Fortune 500 companies came to the campus towards the end of the second year with recruitment in mind. I had no interest in this and was now keenly looking forward to getting back to Ireland. However, a number of approaches were made to me and one in particular stands out. Together with a small number of my classmates I was invited to a lunch hosted by Walter Wriston, President of the American banking colossus, Citibank. Shortly afterwards I had a high-level contact from Citibank offering me a job which would entail my being appointed to run their Irish operations on the basis that they would repay the Bank of Ireland the costs of my time at Harvard. There were a few others in the class of 1970 whose tuition fees had been sponsored by a major company but unlike me, they had a contract to remain with the sponsoring company for at least two years, after which it was understood that it would then be up to the sponsoring firm to retain their services by prospects and pay.

It was a slow dawning thing, but I was beginning to think seriously about where I stood in relation to ethics in business. Although the Harvard Business School did not at that time have specific courses which addressed the issue of business ethics, many of the business policy courses did inevitably pose this question in the context of considering alternative business strategies. I remember, in particular, a case study conducted towards the end of the term by Professor George Lodge, son of Henry Cabot Lodge, who had been a US Vice-Presidential nominee and US Ambassador to Vietnam during the war years. The case dealt with a company in the Philippines at a time when the working-class Filipino population was exceptionally poor, and the issue in the case revolved around the efforts by a group of well-heeled businessmen to 'screw the last peso out of the Filipino' on the one hand, and another group, particularly including the Catholic Church whose objective it was to enhance social democracy within the country and improve the lot of the Filipino peasant. The class was split in two, we were shouting at each other, and five minutes before the end George Lodge strode out of the room with a big grin on his face, knowing he had driven us all to reflect on a very important issue. My sympathies were very much with the working-class Filipinos.

Around this time I began to reflect on what the Harvard Business School experience meant to me. My technical skills in a whole variety of areas such as accountancy, financial control, statistics and business planning had been greatly enhanced, and I felt comfortable that I was familiar with state-of-the-art approaches in these disciplines. I felt that Harvard had provided me over the two-year period with an opportunity to test myself against some of the best and brightest young men and women and I had performed well in this high-powered environment. Most importantly, and I'm not sure this applied to all my classmates; I had learned the important distinction between planning a business strategy and implementing it. My experiences over these couple of years encouraged me to think that I had the capacity to lead and to inspire others to follow. The test of all of this was soon to come in the real world.

At the end of the year we went on a short yachting holiday with one of our classmates, and then it was time to come home. Around this time, the Bank of Ireland's Personnel Department in Dublin contacted me to let me know that all Irish bank staff were now again on strike. It was decided that my circumstances warranted an exemption from taking strike action, though I was still a member of the Union, and the CEO proposed that I should stay on in the United States and investigate the prospects for the Bank of Ireland in the American market. Our good friend, Tom Flatley and his wife, Charlotte, kindly loaned us their holiday home in Cape Cod, and from there I began working enthusiastically on this interesting assignment.

Shockingly, during my time at Harvard there were a number of suicides, including a member of the faculty. To this day I am convinced that a significant contributory factor to these disturbing occurrences was the intensity of work pressure at the school. Towards the end of the second year I arranged a meeting with Dean Lawrence Fouraker to give him feedback on my experience at the Business School. I wanted to raise two points. The first was about the suicides which I attributed to the classroom pressures. I thought that it would be advisable for the School to find ways to reduce the intensity of competition. Mindful of my experience with the Jesuits at Belvedere College, I also criticised the fact that Harvard Business School lacked an appropriate moral compass; there was, for example, no commitment to the community or to social and ethical values. I think I got a good hearing from Dean Fouraker, and coincidentally the lack of attention to ethics and social responsibility was, in part, remedied in the later 1970s through the introduction of a broad range of courses on minority and environmental topics.

The American journal *International Business Week* ran a cover story in 1990 about how our class of 1970 was different to begin with, and how the group turned out. We were a product of an ambitious effort to dramatically increase class diversity and as Tony Athos, the admissions director, said, '*We looked for people who stirred the pot rather than guarded it. The world was changing and it was time for Harvard to change*'. Looking back I think we were a wind of change.

WHAT THEY SAW AT THE REVOLUTION: HARVARD B-SCHOOL'S CLASS OF 1970 WASN'T LIKELY TO FOLLOW CONVENTION. IT DIDN'T

The School now puts a heavy emphasis on contributions to society. It is focused on a more sophisticated definition of capitalism, one that is imbued with social purpose alongside wealth creation. The new conviction is that long-term economic value can best be achieved in collaboration with community and societal needs through processes such as environmental protection, empowering suppliers and investing in education.

Harvard is not alone in rethinking capitalism but through the courses it offers and the research and writing of its professors it is a leader in this. The central role of creativity and innovation in modern capitalism is now addressed in many ways at the Business School, for example through the establishment of 'innovation hubs' and by a greater focus on researching entrepreneurship. Collaborative approaches are now taking centre stage with the constituent schools of Harvard College, including the Business School, the Law School, and the Engineering School. The aim now is to work together in an integrated way, rather than, as in the past, in silos with vested interests hindering progress. Perhaps most importantly, some of the faculty is now focused on the issue of how competition in the capitalist system is being stifled by an unhealthy relationship between government and vested interests. This results in rules which favour already dominant companies and interest groups. More than anything else this process is under-mining the essential feature of the capitalist system, namely, competition. It is stifling innovation, preserving the status quo and inevitably results in an increase in inequality.

The great question I was left with during my life was how the tight, unadventurous, controlled banking world that my father and I remembered back in the 1950s subsequently morphed into the frenzied short-term profit-seeking that resulted in the banking crash decades later. This is a topic I will return to.

Chapter 5

Bank of Ireland Goes Overseas

We arrived home from our more than two-year stint in America in November 1970. Nobody had given me any indication of what I would be doing or who I would be reporting to so there was keen anticipation but also a degree of trepidation.

The six-month bank strike had finally come to an end on 17 November. The background to the strike had its roots in the Irish government's budget of 1968 which resulted in a significant increase in the cost of living during 1969 and 1970. While other employees, including craft and construction workers, secured pay increases of 20 per cent, the banks refused to concede similar increases for their officials. The Irish Bank Officials' Association introduced a work to rule in protest in February 1970. The banks responded by cutting staff salaries by 25 per cent and employing temporary staff. When problems began to emerge in the clearing departments, all staff were suspended in these areas with the result that the banks closed down on 30 April and did not re-open until November.

While the settlement terms mirrored other negotiated settlements of the time, the shutdown of the banking sector for over six months formed a dramatic breakpoint between the old and new styles of banking. The assurances which had been given to the constituent banks at the time of the mergers were broken. The written guarantees negotiated with the Union that no one's promotion prospects or job security would be jeopardised were now ignored. The unit banks' names and management were to disappear. All branches of the constituent banks were to be styled Bank of Ireland branches and, over time, some of these would be closed to achieve economies. What most had feared would now come to pass, the staff from one unit bank was now to work in the same office as staff from another unit bank, and the character and identity of all three banks would be no more.

After the strike a massive cleanup was necessary at the branches and within the administration functions at Head Offices; very welcome overtime money would be earned by staff for many months to come. A significantly more benign environment prevailed at Group Headquarters. By now I had been assured that I was still assigned as an assistant to Dermot Shanley, the Director of Planning. Shanley was a remarkable man; highly intelligent, he had a natural gravitas and leadership aura, was always unhurried and calm and was a great delegator. Colleagues in the Planning Department at the time included Pat Molloy and Maurice Keane, both of whom were to serve with distinction in later years as CEOs of the Bank. Pat, in particular, had an illustrious career. Following his retirement from Bank of Ireland he took on the Chairmanship of CRH Holdings Ltd and then in 2008, in a public-spirited gesture, he accepted the request of the Minister for Finance of the day to go back to the Bank of Ireland which was in considerable financial trouble at the time to take on the Group Chairmanship.

Some days after my return home, I was invited to the office of Frank O'Rourke, one of the General Managers. Frank was a career banker with the Group, an able and popular man who was known for his keen interest in the arts and sports. He was to be responsible for the switchover to decimalisation within the Group and in due course would become the Chief General Manager. For some reason he did not approve of me; at least this is how it seemed to me. Frank congratulated me on my success at Harvard and warmly welcomed me home. He then made what I considered to be an outrageous suggestion, namely, that I should take up the position of Second Assistant Manager at the Bank of Ireland's flagship office in College Green, which he said would provide me with a good opportunity to show everyone what I had learned. I'm not sure what authority he had to make such a proposal, but in any event I turned it down.

The following day I was summoned to the office of the Group Chief Executive, Ian Morrison. Ian was an unusually cerebral man who had been persuaded to give up his accountancy practice and take on the CEO role by the legendary Governor of the bank, Don Carroll. Keyna and I had known him socially in Boston, while he was attending the Advanced Management Program at the Harvard Business School. He was austere, remote, and formal but above all he was a man of action and he played a significant role in modernising Irish banking. The principal purpose of our meeting was to consider the document which I had submitted on the strategic prospects for the Bank of Ireland Group in the United

States. This lengthy document considered a variety of possible locations and it provided detailed commentary on business prospects, regulatory requirements and linkages with Ireland; but most importantly it was a roadmap for the eventual establishment of a full-scale branch banking operation in the United States, with the initial step being the setting up of a New York-based representative office.

He liked the report and told me that it was his intention to bring it to his Executive Committee for consideration. At that stage he introduced me to Bill Finlay, who unknown to me, had been sitting in the wings and listening to our conversation. Finlay, who was at that time a prominent member of the Irish Bar, was to become the next Governor of the Bank's Court of Proprietors. As to the future, it was explained to me that they were now preoccupied with the various problems left by the bank strike. For the moment the best thing for me to do was to conduct a study in the UK along similar lines to the one which I had undertaken in the US. First, however, they wanted me to help in rationalising the many and costly bank accounts which the constituent banks of the Group had with a variety of financial institutions in the City of London.

Before starting on this project I was to undertake an interesting assignment. Because I had had first-hand exposure to the case-study method at Harvard it was suggested that I would prepare such a study on the recent history of the Bank, and in particular its staff relations. The idea was to encourage discussion and debate in the hope of getting a better understanding of the errors of the past. I was given considerable assistance in accessing archival material and I supplemented this with some analysis of my own, designed to help me in leading the case-studies.

Using the Freudian approach I had learned from Harry Levinson one of my notes starts off by referring to: *'The authoritarian style of management which has been predominant in Irish business is largely derived from the concept of authority in the family of a generation ago'.* I went on: *'The merger was a betrayal by the "Father Figure", it was particularly painful that the betrayal was by the Bank of Ireland whose value system crossed religious and nationalistic boundaries. Many people chose to withdraw rather than try to accommodate themselves to a situation where they were now dependent on an unknown institution which had a very different history and traditions. The staff union grew in strength as the conflict with loyalty values diminished. In many cases open hostility caused negative and destructive responses and efforts at communication were largely unsuccessful because the messages were evaluated in terms of their source, rather than their content. The trend towards a more effective style of management was seen as a threat to the omnipotence of senior management. Bank staffs were asked to look at themselves more as businessmen than professionals and this was at variance with their self-image. Great difficulty was experienced in adapting to more democratic leadership tenets and greater decision-making power. The degree of reaction was inverse with years of service. It was most natural that senior personnel would fight anything that sought to prove that their values were poor and the methods they used were wrong. It was equally natural that the young people who had nothing to lose identified positively with change. For the future: the immediate consideration must be the development of trust'.*

Looking back at this document today reminds me of the pain experienced back in those days by so many at all levels. This was not just in the Bank of Ireland Group but also within the AIB Group and the other banks.

My initial visit to the City of London was led by Robin Savage, then Secretary to the Bank. At the time London was a hub for the world's premier banks for currency and bond trading and was the centre for the discount houses. The unit banks within the Bank of Ireland Group were significant depositors with these discount houses. They were the primary focus of our visit, and we soon discovered that they had an unusual and somewhat alarming habit of producing the gin bottle at about 11 a.m. then retiring to lunches which could be prolonged indefinitely by amiable conversation, accompanied by the passing of the port. They were engaging and affable people who appreciated the profitable business they got from Bank of Ireland and no doubt suspected that our visit heralded some reduction of this. I produced a report for the group CEO which recommended a fairly severe restructuring and curtailment of these deposit balances, holding out the prospect of a saving of about £1 million over the next five years.

In developing a presence for the Bank of Ireland in the UK I saw as an obvious first step the establishment of a branch banking network in those parts of the UK where there was a strong Irish connection. Indeed this would do no more than reverse the decision of the National Bank to sell its UK branch banking network at the time of the merger with Bank of Ireland, which many had seen as one of the great financial blunders of the time. Williams and Glyn's Bank had acquired all of this business, together with its clearing bank status, for less than £10 million! But before we did that I suggested that we should focus initially on the establishment of a full-service branch based in the London financial district. I was encouraged to proceed along these lines.

Although there were similarities with the New York study, there was one significant difference. The recommendation to establish a representative office in New York was relatively risk-free notwithstanding high start-up costs; it could be justified based on the opportunity to establish early contact with the many American companies who were planning to locate subsidiaries in Ireland. In the case of the UK the recommendation was for a full-service London City branch. This, however, would inevitably be both costly and risky in terms of the requirements for capital, liquidity, and not least staffing. A very positive feature in support of my recommendation was the strong encouragement from the Bank of England, who was enthusiastic about Bank of Ireland having a presence in the City.

I went to great pains in my proposal to cover the key issues of regulatory requirements, taxation, capital, liquidity and staffing; and not least the business prospects. I had prepared a draft business plan. I duly submitted the plan and waited for a reaction. It was positive but guarded. Countless in-house meetings followed at various levels and with the different departmental interests, and through this process the proposals were refined and improved. Eventually, broad agreement to the plan emerged and the proposals were approved in principle, subject to final sign-off by the Board.

I was to make the presentation of the proposals in the Board Room at the top floor of the Bank's headquarters on College Green. This was the biggest and most important presentation of my life so far. I had rehearsed it in the executive management forum and I felt comfortable and confident on the technical issues involved. However, I was somewhat intimidated facing this audience of the merchant princes of Dublin at the time. Following on the aftermath of the distressing bank strike some of them might (understandably) take the view that this was the wrong time for such a brave initiative. I had no opportunity to rehearse my proposals at this august venue and to my shock when the lights were turned down for my presentation we were put into semi-darkness; I could not read my notes. I had a moment of real panic. Recovering shakily, I asked for lights to be turned up, made what felt like a good presentation, and waited for a reaction. I remember looking out at the audience of the Bank's Directors, catching the eye of Professor James Meenan and recalling my experiences with him at UCD. I had been expecting questions, even opposition and negative views but all I got was silence. Ian Morrison intervened and suggested that some of the members of the Court might like to express their views. And then, one after another these gentlemen voiced their approval of the plans. In particular, Mr. Prendergast, of National Bank heritage, was pleased at the prospect of revisiting the earlier decision to sell the National Bank branches in the UK.

The proposals were then formally approved and accorded priority status. I was really proud of my role in shepherding this important project through all the decision stages. It seemed to me that the City of London was where the world of banking really came alive and my experience at Harvard encouraged me to think on a global scale. In career terms this was the first thing I really wanted, to be in charge of starting up and building the Bank of Ireland's London operations. I did not formally apply for the job but I'm sure it was known that I was interested and expected to be considered. I was not appointed. A Bank of Ireland man, Eamon Simons, was chosen. I was devastated; I was not even interviewed. Ian Morrison bumped into me outside the lift some time later and I recall him commenting to me that they felt the need to appoint a more experienced man and that was that.

Shortly afterwards the Board approved the decision to establish a representative office in New York, with a view to a possible upgrading of this status at a later date. I was asked to go to New York with Pat O'Hara, the appointed representative, to help with the opening of the office and to introduce him to my contacts.

I made it clear that I had no wish to spend any more than a few months in New York but was happy to do this, and once again our family made its way to the U.S.A. Pat, an enthusiastic and talented man, quickly came to grips with the New York business scene and

Opening of the Bank of Ireland's Representative Office in New York. L-R: Pat O'Hara, John Ryan (Governor of the bank), Paddy McEvoy and Monica Conway.

with the possibilities for strengthening Bank of Ireland's presence in the American market. Our principal focus was on the increasing amount of corporate business which was coming from the US to Ireland following the efforts of the Industrial Development Authority (IDA). These were halcyon days for inward investment and huge opportunities existed to form an initial relationship with those US companies planning to locate in Ireland. We also saw ourselves as having an ambassadorial role for Ireland in America.

Together with others from the Embassy, from the Tourist Board, the Export Board, and from institutions like Aer Lingus and CIE, we did our best to promote an image of a modernising and sophisticated Irish economy and indeed the country in general.

When it suited their purpose the IDA would occasionally invite us to join them when they were making a pitch to a potential multinational investor in Ireland. This was not a case of preferring the Bank of Ireland; it was simply a recognition that we were the only bank in town. Our role at these meetings was to provide a private sector view of how modern Ireland embraced the free enterprise ethic and was encouraging to foreign direct investment. I remember an occasion when the Minister for Enterprise, Justin Keating, was in New York on a trade and investment mission and we were invited to join him and the IDA in a meeting with the senior management of a significant American multinational. Justin Keating was a Labour minister in the coalition government and was well-known for his socialist views. In addressing the meeting he passionately extolled Ireland's commitment to the free enterprise economy, he sounded like a genuine capitalist. When he sat down he turned to me and with a wan smile on his face said, *'Can you tell me when I am going to be able to stop prostituting myself like this'*?

All of this led to close friendship with exceptional men such as Joe Malone of Bórd Fáilte and David Kennedy, then Aer Lingus's man in America. Inevitably, there were visits from dignitaries to our handsome suite of offices in the Seagram Building on Park Avenue. There was one occasion when Pat O'Hara and I were hosting a dinner at one of the fashionable New York restaurants for Joe and Imelda Malone. Joe was a close friend of Charles J. Haughey and he invited him to join us at the dinner. We did not know about this until they arrived at the restaurant together. Haughey had just been cleared in the Arms Trial case and the principal purpose of his US visit was to spend time with Ted Kennedy and other members of the Kennedy clan. When he joined our party I had the impression he was somewhat inebriated. In choosing the wine I went for a sufficiently expensive vintage, costing around $25 a bottle. Charlie leaned over and took the wine list from me, perused it in a casual manner and announced that he had found *'An amusing little Château Lafitte, 1961'* (at the outrageous price of $103 per bottle) and that he felt it would be a good idea to order several of these, which we did, and I have regretted it ever since.

Several days later Joe Malone was to host a memorable dinner party at the St. Regis Hotel. It was a fundraiser for a young Irishman, Tony O'Donohue, who was expected to be the next mayor of Toronto, Canada. Haughey was one of the guests. It was one of those parties you remember for the rest of your life because of the ambience, the people, and the conversation. Towards the end of the dinner Joe stood up and said something along the lines of, *'Friends, we must not forget that the purpose of this evening is to honour a great Irish man who is shortly to become the next mayor of Toronto in the great country of Canada. I will now call on Tony to say a few words to us'.*

The *'next mayor of Toronto'* stood up and regaled us for about 45 minutes on such things as secondary and tertiary sewage systems in Toronto and the party fell as flat as a pancake. After coffee, we were all wandering around, joining in different groups and saying things like, *'What a guy, great speech of his'*. At one point I joined a small group of guests which included C. J. Haughey. Somebody repeated the mantra, *'What a guy, what a great speech'* and C. J. responded with, *'I thought it was a load of shit'*. There was a stunned silence and then somebody else said, *'You're absolutely right'*.

In fact Tony O'Donohue failed in his bid to be elected as mayor of Toronto. He lost again in 1978 but his legacy has prevailed. Paul V. Godfrey, Former Chairman, and Municipality of Metropolitan Toronto called him *'The true pioneer of environmental issues in municipal politics in Canada. He made it a key issue many years before the public considered it important. Canadians owe him a true debt of gratitude'*.

After a number of months in New York, it was time to come home again. We had been living in Rye, which is situated along the New Haven line to Connecticut, and during my last week in New York it happened that Jack Stanley, the General Manager in charge of overseas operations, was staying at our house. The Bank had been hoping at the time to conclude some business with one of the premier Mexican state-companies, and Jack proposed that I go to Mexico before going home with a view to concluding this. I had superb introductions for this visit: Jack gave me a letter of introduction to Rómulo O'Farrill Junior, a billionaire Mexican, who happened to be the Honorary Consul General for Ireland and Joe Malone gave me an introduction to Stephanie, who had been a former Aer Lingus hostess and was now married to Lorenzo, a renowned Mexican sculptor and the man who had designed the medals for the 1968 Olympic Games. These Games are mainly remembered for two remarkable events: Bob Beamon won the long jump by extraordinarily jumping almost two feet beyond the world record, and a man called Fosbury won the high jump by jumping backwards! We stayed in the wondrous Camino Real Hotel which had been specially built for these Olympics.

The introduction to Señor O'Farrill turned out to be productive beyond my expectations; from day one of our short stay he put a chauffeur-driven car at my disposal and then he arranged for one-on-one meetings with the chief executives of the top half dozen Mexican companies. The O'Farrill surname originated in Ireland and Romulo O'Farrill Junior was a member of the seventh generation of the family name. He was a kingmaker in Mexico; immensely wealthy, owning commercial TV stations and newspapers as well as car distribution agencies. During the course of my visit he arranged for me to be interviewed about Ireland and the Irish economy by the top Mexican daily newspaper. This interview gave me an opportunity to laud the industrial progress that was taking place in Ireland at the time. My visit was described in the newspaper as being, *'An investigation of the possibilities for Bank of Ireland representation in Mexico'*.

Banker Cites Industrial Boom

"THE NEWS" MEXICO CITY, SATURDAY, JANUARY 15, 1972.

Irish Image Updated

Patrick C. McEvoy. . . Bank of Ireland

I had at this stage reached agreement with Pemex, the State oil company, for the Bank of Ireland to provide a $20 million term loan and coincidental with my business agenda I had also made contact with Stephanie and Lorenzo. They were a wonderful outgoing friendly couple who went to great trouble to show us some of Mexico's history and countryside. We visited ancient Aztec ruins in towns like Cuernavaca and Cuerna. Keyna and I subsequently called our holiday home in Wexford 'Cuerna'.

A few days before we were due to go home Señor O'Farrill invited us to lunch at his home. It was an enormous mansion, mostly built in marble, with a garage outside for 20 cars, including Lamborghinis, Porsches, and Maseratis. The entrance to the courtyard was protected by armed guards and dogs. Internally the furniture was Louis XIV style. His wife apologised straight away that the normal complement of ten staff were on their day off and apparently we would have to make do with only three serving people. At the end of a very enjoyable lunch, O'Farrill said that he was aware that we would be leaving in a few days and, if my business was completed, he would like to put one of his executive jets at our disposal to take us to his holiday home in Acapulco on the following day. Clumsily, I told him that we had already been invited out by Stephanie and Lorenzo and that therefore we would have to decline his kind invitation (Keyna has never fully forgiven me for this). There is however, a footnote to the story. Our friends took us to a restaurant called Fondo del Ricardo, which was a great favourite with the locals. It was very basic and cheap with linoleum on the tables, but the meal was accompanied by the most wonderful mariachi singing and we were served the best red snapper I have ever experienced. A few years ago, I read a piece in *The Irish Times* which described the best restaurants in Mexico City. Number one on the list was Fondo del Ricardo.

Things had been moving at a frantic pace back home in Dublin. The management consulting firm McKinsey's assignment with Bank of Ireland had continued for several years. Initially, they proposed centralised operations and now they changed tack and suggested decentralised structures. I don't know whether this was all part of a grand plan or whether there had been a genuine change of heart. Included in their recommendations was the creation of a new Corporate and Overseas Department. Jack Stanley was the General Manager of this new division. His letter to me in the spring of 1972 said:

'The Managing Director today appointed you to be Chief Corporate Account Manager, Europe within the overseas department. The job carries the full status of Assistant General Manager and all the perks that go with this'. I was absolutely elated by this news; it made all the hard work worthwhile.

Jack Stanley and Maurice Keane.

Jack had been recruited from Citibank, where he had been running their Irish operations. In the course of the lunch hosted during my Harvard days by Walter Wriston, Citibank's President, he had told me privately about Jack's move to Bank of Ireland. He said they were very sorry to see him go and had expected that he would go far in Citibank's management hierarchy.

Jack Stanley was a natural leader, a 'can-do' man, and intensely loyal to his colleagues. Working with him was one of the great delights and learning experiences of my life. I made countless overseas trips with him to European banks or to potential clients for the Bank of Ireland. Jack always wanted to make seven appointments a day and I would say: *'Jack, you can't do that; we will never be able to fit them in'*, to no avail. He was so popular that inevitably these meetings took longer than anticipated. At the end of the second meeting we were usually cancelling the last meeting, and at the end of the third meeting we were cancelling the second last meeting.

Our business in 'Overseas' was principally about developing banking relationships with overseas companies who were locating in Ireland. The new multinational business in Ireland was the beginning of a transformation in the economy; in terms of jobs, in exports, and in our confidence to compete on the world stage. Much of this foreign direct investment was located outside Dublin and it had a profound impact on the regeneration of rural economies. It also had a significant effect on the profit performance of the local bank branches in terms of high-quality lending, foreign exchange business and, not least, growth in personal current account and savings account volumes. We were very successful in our efforts to win business in competition with the AIB Group. We had a great operational structure at the time with representation in London,

New York and now also Frankfurt. This was personally very satisfying work.

I felt it was capitalism at its best, capitalism with a social purpose. These were very happy years for me. I was very conscious of my debt to Harvard Business School for all the good fortune that I was now experiencing in my career. HBS gave me the tools, improved capacity for critical thinking, and not least, self-confidence.

A meeting of the Harvard Business School of Ireland Club in the early 1970's.

Around this time I took on the presidency of the Irish Harvard Business School Club. This was a year-long assignment during which we had two future Nobel Laureates among our guest speakers, John Hume and Seamus Heaney. As my life progressed I was to stay in touch with Harvard and with former classmates and attend some class reunions.

In the late spring of 1973 I was holidaying with my family in north-western Scotland when I happened to read a small advertisement in the *Financial Times* about a new bank to be established in Ireland where the promoters were seeking to recruit a founding chief executive. On enquiry, it transpired that the ownership behind the proposed new venture, while disparate, did have a significant minority holding by one of the largest banks in the world, the US Marine Midland Bank.

I was very happy working with the Bank of Ireland Group at that time. As an Assistant General Manager I had status, I was well paid, and the work was socially productive and personally fulfilling. Nonetheless, when I saw this ad for the CEO of a start-up Irish bank and I did see the significance of the shareholding support from an institution such as Marine Midland Bank, quite simply my heart beat faster and I had to make further enquiries. This struck me at the time as being possibly the type of opportunity which would never, ever, happen again. I fully appreciated that the situation I was in with Bank of Ireland provided me with great security and that a venture such as this would be full of risk and uncertainty. However, I felt secure in my own abilities and reasoned that, given my background, age, and qualifications, I was eminently employable.

I went to see the founding Chairman, Donal McAleese, at what was to be the headquarters of the new Bank, situated in a lovely old four-storey building at 91 Merrion Square. One of the big things I

123

had going for me was that Donal McAleese was a fellow Belvederian, albeit of a different vintage. There was simply an immediate sense of trust and rapport based on our shared experience of schooling with the Jesuits. I made it quite clear to him that I really wanted the job. About the interviews, Donal was subsequently quoted as saying: *'He was very bold about it. He rang me as well as putting in a written application for the job. I like to remind him that he interviewed me on the phone instead of the other way round. I tried telling him at the time, this was not the way things were done, old boy, but he didn't bother about any of that which was just as well for us'.*

I asked him about the shareholders' plan but there was no plan, other than to make money. I suggested to him that the proposed name of Irish Intercontinental Bank (IIB) Ltd might be a bit presumptuous, he disagreed. I asked about staffing and was told that there had been offers 'in principle' to a number of individuals but that it was anticipated that the CEO when appointed would have an opportunity to take his own view of the calibre of these people. Apparently, the initial capitalisation of the new bank was to be at a very modest level, initial capital of £1 million, with 50 per cent of that paid up. Donal stressed that there would be unstinting support from the American shareholder through their London subsidiary. It was suggested that the next step would be for me to visit London to meet with Charlton McVeagh Junior and his executive colleagues at the premises of the International Marine Banking Company in London.

Charlie McVeagh, a cultured, understated Bostonian, explained to me at the outset that his Bank had been given a mandate by their American parent to aggressively develop an international banking presence in the City of London. He was joined at the meeting by his executive colleagues including Derek Foote, Ian McLeish, and a young South African lawyer named Richard Fenhalls. I remember commenting to Charlie that he wore both *'belt and braces'* and my asking him as to whether there was any significance in this, he liked that. This was by no means a stress interview, indeed I got the impression that they were also trying to impress me. Their commitment to the new Irish institution was most impressive; for example, Charlie told me that it was their intention to give the new Irish entity a sizeable and fully funded Eurodollar portfolio which would cover early costs and hopefully generate a small profit for the first year's operations.

A few weeks later, Donal contacted me and offered me the position of Managing Director, to be confirmed as CEO after a short period of time. I accepted. Those years from 1973 to my retirement as Chairman in 2005 were my happiest and most fulfilling. This was to be my life's major work.

It was a huge wrench for me to leave the Bank of Ireland. I was also very conscious of my indebtedness to them for their investment in my education. Several things were relevant for me here: I knew that the norm in the US was a formal obligation to work with the sponsoring company for no more than two years in the case of full-time financial support to MBA level programmes. More importantly, I believed that the contributions that I had made to the Bank since my return from Harvard were a good return on their investment in me. However, I was still concerned as to how it would be perceived by my employer. To my relief Ian Morrison called me to his office and told me that I had made a valuable contribution and that I left with goodwill and good wishes. Jack Stanley as always was marvelous, he took the initiative in organising a send-off for me and at the party he said lots of complimentary things.

Life moved on for me into the area of the known and the unknown unknowns.

Chapter 6

Irish Intercontinental Bank
The Early Years

The opportunity to establish Irish Intercontinental Bank Ltd came about because an existing Dublin bank (Irish International Bank), operating out of 91 Merrion Square, was reaching the end of its commercial life. It had been set up ten years earlier, in 1963, and listed some interesting names among its shareholders. These included Princess Palavi, the sister of the Shah of Iran, the TV personality Eamonn Andrews, and the future Lord Mayor of Dublin, Ben Briscoe TD. Under its managing director, Charles Parnell, the bank had hit problems and had been put into receivership. The receiver was Lawrence Crowley; this was one of his first receiverships in a long and distinguished career.

After talks with the Central Bank, the banking regulator agreed to give the Dunkeld Holdings/International Marine Banking Co. Ltd joint-venture a merchant banking licence. The initial shareholding structure included a 10 per cent holding for a Bostonian named Blake, who had played a role in putting the deal together. In return for the licence, the new venture undertook to repay creditors of Irish International Bank. A deal was done with the receiver of Irish International Bank whereby, in return for a banking licence and a fine premises located beside the National Gallery of Ireland, some

127

£250,000 would be paid for the assets and £125,000 would be paid towards the creditors of the old bank.

A number of staff had already been recruited, including John Kelly, initially in charge of the administration function, and Donal's secretary, Hannah Crowley. I was a fortunate man as both John and Hannah were exceptional employees and were of inestimable value to us over the years. Donal McAleese was at the time President of the Federated Union of Employers. He was widely respected in the business community and seemed to know everyone. Over the years of working with him, I particularly came to appreciate his qualities of integrity and courage, and not least his laconic sense of humour. In early course Donal's immediate tasks were to finalise the banking licence with the Central Bank and to put the local Board of Directors in place. The initial list of directors was, I felt, impressive including people like Ted O'Boyle (retired CEO of the Ulster Bank), Geoffrey Wilson (retired CEO of British Rail), Donal Roche (co-founder with his brother Tom of Cement Roadstone Holdings (CRH)) and several senior executives from International Marine Banking Co. Ltd. (Intermarine). The banking licence was finalised in the spring of 1973 and we opened our doors for business in October of that year.

I had no idea what we were going to do. But though I didn't have a plan I did have an attitude and philosophy. I wanted to play a role in building a bank which would emphasise the highest ethical standards and contribute to the community.

The first board of Irish Interconental Bank: from left Geoffrey Wilson, Charlton McVeagh, Frank Blake, Richard Fenhalls, Donal McAleese, Paddy McEvoy, Jim Doolan, Donal Roche and Ted O'Boyle.

I felt that this was an opportunity to change the status quo in the sector and in particular challenge the dominance of Bank of Ireland and AIB in corporate banking. To achieve this we aimed to bring tailor-made banking services to the customer instead of waiting for the customer to come to the bank. But I had no idea how we were going to do this and no particular thoughts on what services we might offer.

So, the first steps were to set up the company and then figure out what to do with it. We needed the right people, the right business structures and a willingness to experiment. People would be the key. I was looking for people who had high professional

129

competence; but who were also comfortable with being uncomfortable, shades of Harvard's Tony Athos and his mantra that life's great certainties were *'uncertainty, ambiguity, and imperfection'*, and who had curiosity and the humility to change tack.

Ted Marah was one of our first recruits, coming from the state-owned Industrial Credit Corporation. This was one of the great pieces of good fortune we had. Ted's influence on the bank over the years was seminal and in due course he took over from me as CEO.

Our first requirement was to establish an earnings flow, and it was agreed that Intermarine would provide us with an $8 million fully funded portfolio of international loans. These included things like 2 per cent of a large bulk carrier, 1 per cent of an airliner, and 5 per cent of the Shah of Iran's bonds, which were 'triple A rated' at the time. Initially, no indemnity was offered on this portfolio. I asked Ted to review the loans for us and, following on this, we decided that we would not take the loans unless they were guaranteed by Intermarine. Thankfully, this indemnity was forthcoming; otherwise the financial crisis of 1973-75 would have sunk the bank before it began.

Our first accounts produced in the spring of 1974 declared a profit of a few hundred pounds. By 2005, the year I retired from the chairmanship of the bank, the combined profitability of the group's operations was in excess of €200 million.

The big problem from the very beginning was the difficulty in raising deposits which could facilitate lending. This led to the early emphasis on investment-type banking such as corporate finance transactions, and the search for opportunities to take an equity position. An early example of the latter was the case of J. V. McDaniel Ltd. Jim Flavin had started Development Capital Corporation Ltd (DCC) at around the same time as our bank was founded, and their initial focus was the provision of capital in return for equity stakes. McDaniel's was one of the companies they invested in, and our payback for the provision of term bank finance was a minority equity stake.

The unwillingness of other banks and financial institutions to lend to us was understandable, we had a very low level of capital, we lacked an earnings history, and the diverse structure of our shareholding did not inspire confidence. Worse was to follow. As happens in the business world, a seemingly unconnected event was to have very far-reaching consequences, not just for our bank but for the Irish and the global economy. The OPEC countries decided to use the so-called oil weapon and drastically increase the price of crude oil. In the very year our bank was founded, the Yom Kippur War precipitated the first oil crisis and that, together with the secondary banking collapse in the UK, plunged the West into recession. By late 1974, the ripple effect was continuing. The price of oil had quadrupled, interest rates were rising and Irish and UK conglomerate companies with large property exposures were being badly hit, sometimes terminally. Unfortunately for IIB, one of those taking a direct hit was Intermarine in London, which had large property investments and was teetering on the edge of bankruptcy.

In Dublin, Dunkeld Holdings, which had a strong link to the property market, was not faring much better and was also reaching a stage where it would need to be bailed out. The net effect of all of this was that the fledgling IIB was a small bank caught in the middle of two troubled shareholders, though making small but respectable money.

Those days were truly entrepreneurial for us. The problems being experienced by both our institutional shareholders inevitably led to a dramatic shareholder restructuring at IIB. The state-owned insurance company, Irish Life, now had a direct 25 per cent interest together with a further indirect holding through their part ownership of Dunkeld, with the balance now being owned directly by Intermarine's US parent, the Marine Midland Bank. Donal McAleese and I went to New York to talk to Marine Midland about their future intentions for us, when we were told that they had no interest in continuing with a direct shareholding of 31 per cent in an Irish bank.

We clearly needed a long-term solution to the bank's shareholding problems but in the meantime I felt very positive that the effective majority shareholder was a state-owned insurance company, with the balance being held by a major American bank. In due course, given our recent joining in 1973 of the European Union, we could offer an interesting proposition to a significant European bank, one that might see the attraction of buying into an operation in Ireland which was already up and running and staffed by a competent and ambitious young team.

The oil crisis exacted a heavy toll on Dunkeld, which became technically insolvent. Donal McAleese effectively moved out of the bank, although remaining as its Chairman, to help sort out the problems of some of Dunkeld's constituent companies. I had been formally appointed as CEO of IIB in early 1974.

Deposits are the lifeblood of a bank, and I was acutely aware that we could not build profitability unless we had a stable funding base to support lending. We had done some nice corporate finance deals in the first couple of years, including a public offering for the bloodstock agency Goffs, the reintroduction of a well-known Irish drapery store to the Irish stock exchange, and some financial consultancy work for US multinational companies establishing operations in Ireland. We had also managed to sell our shareholding in McDaniel's for a profit of £48,000. We knew however that funding either by way of corporate deposits, or interbank lines, or the discounting of trade bills, was the key. The Executive Committee minutes for 1974 note that we made 90 separate calls to attract deposits, while the 1975 minutes puts this figure at 175.

Donal and I made a number of visits to the City of London with a view to attracting funding support. I remember two such visits in particular. The National Westminster Bank was banker to Irish Life in the UK, and Donal decided that we should visit their Princes Street branch, rather than their Head Office to solicit a money market line. Notwithstanding our fragile circumstances, he was optimistic that the National Westminster Bank would be more than happy to accommodate us. We greatly misread the situation. When we went to the Princes Street branch we found that the Group Treasurer had been summoned from Head Office to attend the meeting. Frankly, they appeared shocked at our request, and sadly no deposit support was forthcoming. I subsequently discovered that a memorandum of the meeting had been prepared and copied to their Irish subsidiary, Ulster Bank which described our approach and expectations as *'incredible'*.

On another occasion we called on one of the blue-blooded discount houses, C. Hoare & Co. with the intention of procuring a line to discount trade bills, these bills would offer security to the discount house both of our bank and the trade name. We were ushered into a cavernous office at the end of which a very well-dressed gentleman sat behind a large polished desk. He did not stand up, he did not greet us, in fact he never moved. We were standing at the far end of the room and Donal, speaking in a tone of voice which could only be heard by me, said, *'Don't say a word'*.

As far as I was concerned, he was the Chairman and, despite my natural inclination to start talking, I held my peace. A protracted staring match ensued and eventually the man from C. Hoare & Co. cracked; he stood up, put out his hand, smiled, and said something along the lines of, *'I appreciate that you will have come from Ireland and would like to establish a line to discount bills with us, that will be no problem, gentlemen'*. That was Donal McAleese at his very best.

After the changes in our shareholding structure in 1975 Ted Marah and I went back to London to test the market with our new story. I suppose we had a nerve given that there had been a collapse of the secondary banking market in the City and that the UK economy was in the throes of a lasting recession. We had befriended two of the general managers in a very significant discount house named Gerrard and National; these gentlemen invited us to lunch with a view to meeting with their Chairman, Lord Jessop, and they were optimistic about the prospects of establishing a banking relationship with us. There was no sign of their Chairman when we arrived and we duly proceeded to lunch in his absence. We were halfway through the lunch when Lord Jessop stumbled in. He never acknowledged us, went straight to the bar and poured himself a large gin. He sat down at the table, wolfed his way through the first course, and then caught up with us in the main course, all of this without a word.

He then took a big swig of his drink, turned to me and said, *'Quite, you are here from Ireland, eh. Tell me, what is the potato crop like this year'*? Ted says that, without batting an eye, I responded with a treatise to the effect that, *'The province of Leinster had a decent year, Munster had an exceptional crop, but Connaught was going through a bad patch'*.

I remember that his two general manager colleagues were mortified, and I honestly don't think that he appreciated that we were taking the micky out of him. We did a lot of discounting business over many years with Gerrard and National and I like to think that, through this process, we introduced them to quality Irish names.

Those early entrepreneurial years were both challenging and fun. The period from late 1973 to the end of 1977 was productive. We had put in place a top-class core management group which would serve the company well for several decades, including Ted Marah, John Kelly, Pat Larragy, and Liam Donlon. The bank had a modest but growing reputation in the domestic corporate finance area and a loan book of good quality. Despite a few wobbles it was gaining momentum but we were still constrained by the difficulties in establishing a reliable funding base.

One of our earlier loans was in the wobble category. We provided a facility of £200,000 to a husband-and-wife film production team, Claude and Catherine Winter. They were French nationals, and the purpose of the facility was to finance the production of a film to be shot at Ardmore Studios in Bray, Co. Wicklow. The film, *The Purple Taxi* (*Un Taxi Mauve*), was based on a book by bestselling and prize-winning author Michel Déon, and had a star-studded cast including Peter Ustinov, Fred Astaire, Charlotte Rampling, and the famous French actor, Philippe Noiret. It seemed like a sure-fire deal for us; we had the security of the film itself as well as the personal guarantees of the Winters.

We had satisfied ourselves that they were people of substance. Sheamus Smith, the boss of Ardmore Studios, was a personal friend of mine, and I had the great good fortune to be invited by him to a small luncheon for the famous Peter Ustinov. It was also attended by the broadcaster, Gay Byrne. The lunch lasted for about five hours and was a tour de force of marvellous raconteurship by

Ustinov, accompanied by his imbibing copious quantities of a quite ordinary red wine. In particular, I remember the hilarious stories he told about the special school that had been set up by the British Secret Service to teach their field staff how to stutter properly.

In due course, the film was completed. French audiences were enthusiastic but unfortunately it was an abject failure in the English-speaking world. When we attempted to get our money back from Catherine and Claude Winter we were met with silence. After a period of time, and conscious that the debt was rolling up because of the unplanned addition of interest due, I went to visit the Winters in Paris. I was informed that they were perfectly happy to repay the debt but that the Banque de France was refusing to give them permission to make the necessary payment. So I went to see the Banque de France. Communication was impossible because the official refused to use the English language and my French was not adequate. I went back to the Winter's and threatened to take legal action to recover our debt, this eventually did the trick. As a bonus I was invited to the official screening of the film at the Cannes Film Festival that year. The Irish group included the broadcaster, Bill O'Herlihy, and the famous harpist Deirdre O'Callaghan. We were all entertained royally at the palatial residence of the Irish consul general, Pierre Joannon, and his lovely wife Annick in the company of glamorous film stars.

In those days we lived in a nice dormer house in South County Dublin; it was close to the sea and we had a very popular hard tennis court in the garden. The sea was a huge attraction for all of us but the commute was increasingly a problem both for me and for Keyna, who had at this stage qualified as a lawyer with an office in the city. We decided to move into town and were willing to bid to the limit of our resources to get a house that we might live in for the rest of our lives. Eventually, we found the house of our dreams at Number 3 Northbrook Road and we determined to make a bid for it. I was banned from attending the auction because Keyna feared that I would exceed our agreed maximum bidding figure of £40,000. In the spring of 1974 we acquired this beautiful Victorian residence at the very limit of our agreed bidding figure. We were to live there for more than 30 years, eventually building a new modern house in part of the garden. As is well known, house prices gyrated crazily in Ireland in subsequent years and when we looked to sell the property in 2005 the asking price was €5 million! It was withdrawn at auction and we eventually sold it for €2 million in 2013. The family grew to love the house at 3 Northbrook Road. Keyna well remembers one special party there:

'It was a shambles when we purchased it but had some beautiful features including a very wide and impressive hallway with a lovely archway and a wonderful mahogany staircase going from the hall to the upper landing, the bannister of which was held in place by decorated wrought iron. The ceilings were 12-14 feet high and had lovely stucco and other ornate details in the hallways and all the main rooms.

Our home at 3 Northbrook Road.

The house was particularly good for large parties, many of which were for customers of the bank, when we would normally engage outside caterers. For more than 20 years every November we used to host a large drinks party for as many as 120 people, our guests used to tell us that they regarded our party as the start of the Christmas season. A special memory I have is the first time we had 'disco' lights for a party. Paddy's mother had come to live with us and we had built a self-contained apartment for her in half our garden level area. She was a small delicate lady and her

139

mobility was now severely restricted by arthritis. She came in to the party on a walking frame to view the room and especially the lights. She had never seen anything like this before and she just stood there in amazement in the middle of all the lights which were swirling, flickering, and dancing off the walls and floors and ceilings, while the music filled not just the room but the whole party area'.

Over these years we enhanced the house with memorabilia acquired on our numerous overseas trips to places like Zimbabwe, South Africa, Prague, Budapest and, memorably, Morocco. Our time in Morocco was short but it did provide me with another lesson in the 'art of salesmanship'.

The souk in Morocco's capital city, Marrakesh, is an unforgettable experience. It is a teeming, sprawling, babble of a market where you can buy anything from a snake to a snake charmer. Our tour guide led us into a rambling area where we were given a demonstration in the arts of carpet making and then shepherded into an even larger emporium groaning with finished carpets. Here we met Abdullah, flowing white robes, pearly teeth, oozing charm, *'I love the Irish. You are such wonderful footballers. My carpets are the finest in the world. It will be my great pleasure to display them. You will not be buying, of course, just looking, and we will remain good friends'.*

Abdullah then clapped his hands and mint tea appeared. Several acolytes started unfurling carpets into three different groupings beside us. *'Which do you prefer? Not to buy, of course, just to look'.*

I motioned to one group. *'Ah, you have such a good eye, for me it is such a pleasure to speak to one who has an eye for beauty, these carpets, you know, they last for 70 years and then you come back and we exchange it for a new one, for free. Price is nothing, quality is all'*. The carpets kept unfurling before our eyes, like a magician taking handkerchiefs from a hat. *'Which size you prefer, which colour, you have perhaps some special place in your house'*?

At this stage I felt compelled to remind Abdullah that we were only there to look, and he got slightly cross with me. *'You must allow me to do my job and not interfere'*. He flashed a magic smile. *'The Irish are so impulsive, I like you, you are my friend, this is your house and you will remain my friend even if you do not buy'*. The hook was slightly into us at this stage and in any event courtesy required that we acknowledge how very beautiful the carpets were. His face was in rapture, *'They are irresistible, no? You would like two of them'*? Abdullah smiled. *'And now I will tell you the prices'*, he said. *'You will see they are very special prices'*. He reeled off a list of prices depending on size and quality. They did indeed seem to us to be good prices. *'Which colours do you prefer'*? demanded Abdullah. *'I have made no decision to purchase'*, I replied. Abdullah gave an exasperated shrug and spread his arms wide, *'Which colour is your choice'*? We consulted. *'I suppose the blue is our favourite'*.

In an unbelievably short time everything that was not blue disappeared from view. There then remained the most gorgeous blue rugs which were all stacked according to size and quality.

'Which quality, which size you prefer'? Abdullah enquired. I remonstrated, he dismissed my remonstrations. *'You must allow me to do my job'*, he said. Abdullah walked away, then turned back and looked me between the eyes. *'Make me an offer'*, he commanded. *'Your best price, I must close up this afternoon and stay closed for two weeks and for this and because I like you, I will give you a very special price'.* 'Abdullah, *my friend'*, I said, *'I have made no decision to purchase and if, as you request, I make you an offer and you accept, then I will feel obliged to purchase'.*

Another trader in the Marrakesh Souk,
could be Abdullah's brother!

At this stage he rephrased himself, *'You will tell me what you think your favourite carpet is worth'*, again the magic smile.

I consulted with Keyna and we suggested a price of considerably less than half the sum he had quoted for a medium-sized, highest quality carpet. *'As an absolute maximum'* I said, feeling sure that this would terminate the proceedings. There was quite a long silence and quite a bit of eyeball to eyeball stuff. *'I accept your offer, this lovely carpet of yours will last forever, and you have made me very happy. We will ship and insure and you will have it in six weeks'.* After the arrangements were completed and bona fides confirmed Abdullah bade us farewell. *'You will not forget to send me the Lacoste T-shirt'* he implored. *'When the carpet arrives Abdullah . . . when the carpet arrives'.* In due course the carpet arrived and looked very beautiful on the floor of our main reception room. The T-shirt (not Lacoste) was dispatched. However, I must say that my preference remains for a softer sell.

Number 3 was where my interest in the game of table tennis flourished. My younger son, Dermot, and I used to play for hours, long after the others had gone to bed. They were ferociously competitive games and I remember that though Dermot was clearly the better player he still could not beat his father. Until one night he did and I never won a match after that.

One of my favourite recollections of the house concerns my nephew and godson Richard Gallagher, now a Major with the United States Army. My younger sister, Helen, and her husband Edward had emigrated to Rhode Island in the 1990s and Richard was their elder son. He arrived at our doorstep one day, without any advance notice and explained that he was on a European tour with a friend and would it be all right if they came in and maybe even stayed for the night. We said that we would be delighted to accommodate them and they could stay as long as they wanted. It transpired that he actually had five friends with him. They all trooped sheepishly into the house. They stayed for several days, sleeping all over the place. A great time was had by all of us, particularly over the meals when wide-ranging discussions took place. Many years later I heard that Richard was accustomed to tell the story that before he prevailed on Paddy and Keyna to provide meals and accommodation for him and his entourage he had 'marked his friends' cards' in the following manner. *'Now listen, lads, when we sit down for dinner you may think it's only a dinner but I have to tell you that Paddy loves to be the chairman and you must behave at the meals as if it was also a meeting of the Board of Directors'*!

By 1977 Marine Midland Bank had told us they were not interested in retaining their minority shareholding, and Irish Life did not wish to retain effective majority control of the bank, so it was my task to find a 75 per cent new owner in order to leave Irish Life with a reduced holding of 25 per cent. Bernard Breen, General Manager of the Central Bank, told me that they wished to see our shareholding restructured and suggested two names, American Express and Kredietbank in Belgium (KB). The idea of having American Express as a majority shareholder never went anywhere, leaving us with Kredietbank, which we knew to be a very powerful bank in its home country. I went to Brussels to meet with Professor Luc Wauters, who was about to move from the Chief Executive role to the Chairmanship of KB and Dr. August Leeman, his designated successor. The preliminary talks went well; they were familiar with

Ireland, having done some bond business with the Irish government and they seemed to like the idea of being involved as a majority owner in an Irish start-up bank. In early course they carried out a due diligence; at that time we had about £19 million in assets and £1 million in paid-up capital together with a couple of hundred thousand pounds in profits. When the due diligence was complete, I was invited over to Brussels for more talks, and subsequently Wauters, Leeman, McAleese, and I agreed everything over dinner in our Northbrook Road house.

IRISH BUSINESS, March, 1978

COVER STORY — JOHN O'NEILL

Talking to Irish Business were, left to right, Corneil Withofs, Executive Director, I.I.B.; Luc Wauters, President, Kredietbank; Paddy McEvoy, Managing Director, I.I.B., and Dr. August Leeman, Managing Director, Kredietbank.

Belgian Bank Attacks
Dublin Market

While the final papers to give effect to these agreements were being prepared, I was to experience a little trial in the Irish Courts system which was to cause me some grief.

One night, after Keyna and I had seen a movie at the Savoy Cinema in Dublin's O'Connell Street, I decided to drive home via

Marlborough Street. The street was deserted as I slowly eased my way through the stop sign at the level crossing opposite Julia's Hot Bread Shop, I will never forget it. A motorcycled Garda came roaring by, missed my car by a few yards, screeched to a stop, parked his bike, and came towards me threateningly, notebook in hand. '*You went through that stop sign without stopping, you could have killed me, and I intend to prosecute you*', he said. I did my best to explain and apologised profusely but he was not for turning. '*You will be hearing from me*' he said, as he rode off.

The period within which a summons must be served in order to commence an action is six months and, on the last day of the six-month period, a uniformed Garda knocked on the door of my house and produced a summons for dangerous driving.

This was a traumatic experience for me; I was involved in starting up a new bank and was in the middle of concluding the most important transaction in my business life to date. I envisaged headlines in the *Evening Herald* along the lines, '*Bank chief convicted of dangerous driving*'. Keyna was at the time a partner in Rowan and Company, a small law firm. Together with the senior partner, Pat Rowan, she engaged Peter Sutherland as my counsel. He was then a very promising junior. On the appointed day, we all turned up at the district court of Justice Delap. The courtroom reminded me of a rural primary school as we sat down to listen to the case being heard before ours. This involved a young man who had behaved in an abusive and belligerent manner to a member of the Garda; and he had elected to defend himself. District Justice

146

Delap was a ruddy-faced man, known to have a quick temper. He was very annoyed by the performance of the defendant and was threatening to inflict the maximum possible penalty. At this stage, Peter Sutherland asked us to join him in the corridor outside the court.

'Paddy, I'm sorry to say that, I think the Judge has lost it and this is very bad news for us, I'm not sure what I can do'. We traipsed back in, disconsolately. Our case was up next for hearing. The young Garda who had accosted me was giving evidence, dispassionately. When he was nearly finished Peter Sutherland stood up and said, *'Your honour, we have just heard of a case where a member of the public treated a member of An Garda Síochána shamefully. Would you mind if I asked the prosecuting Garda to let us know how my client behaved'*? The prosecuting Garda said, *'I have to say that your client behaved like a perfect gentleman'*. *'Case dismissed'* said the Judge!

I have always felt that this was an exquisite piece of legal pleading, and to this day I am grateful to Peter Sutherland, who, as the world knows, was to make major contributions in many fields in Ireland and internationally. There was, however, a small postscript in the matter. When the three of us were walking out of the court, Mr. Justice Delap said, *'Oh, excuse me, Mr. Sutherland, may I enquire as to how much money your client makes a week'*? Peter Sutherland replied that his client was indeed in receipt of a reasonable level of pay. *'Would he like to make a contribution to the Garda Benevolent Association?'* enquired the Judge. I think the amount I handed over was about five pounds. All things considered, I felt I had got a really good deal.

Chapter 7

IIB and How We Built a Bank
Part 1

Kredietbank's acquisition of 75 per cent shareholding in what was now to be called IIB Bank, rather than Irish Intercontinental Bank, was completed in the spring of 1978. They would remain as shareholders until today, buying out the Irish Life minority share in 2002. In 2008 the name was changed again, to KBC Bank Ireland. The new shareholders were impressive; they were enthusiastic about supporting us in every way possible, including increasing our capital funds and providing us with significant expertise and personnel in the foreign exchange area. They also provided a letter of comfort to the Central Bank of Ireland, which was effectively a guarantee of our liabilities. The period of entrepreneurship was well and truly behind us.

I took a short break at the time and happily Keyna was able to join me. In those days we were big into so-called 'venture sports'. We tried all sorts of things, including scuba-diving in the Caribbean and off the Florida coast, as well as an eight-day trip together with former Harvard colleagues rafting the famous Grand Canyon.

But by far the maddest adventure was when we went paragliding in the French Alps. I had been attending a conference in the French town of Talloires, which was situated beside the beautiful Lake Annecy. The conference itself was a very high-powered event with participants including a well-known Russian oligarch, the anchor newsman at CNN, and several CEOs of major banks.

On our last night we dined in a Michelin-starred restaurant, where the topic of conversation at our table came around to paragliding. Because of its location and the panoramic scenery Talloires had become a leading paragliding centre in Europe.

Whitewater rafting on the Colorado River with friends from Harvard days, Bill Allen and Dick Norman.

Me, down but certainly not out on that rafting trip.

During coffee breaks at the conference we could lift our eyes to heaven and see the paragliders like multi-coloured spots in the sky. It was probably the effect of the wine but we all decided that we would meet up the next morning to experience the thrill of paragliding.

Paragliding, the lunacy of jumping off a mountain top.

The following day only two couples showed up, the McEvoys and Susan Pharr, Professor of Japanese Studies at Harvard, with her husband Bob. None of us had any experience so we planned to do what was called a tandem paragliding flight, which would involve jumping off the mountain with a trainer from one of the local schools for a flight which was to last about twenty minutes. We motored up to the top of the mountain, a journey of about twenty five minutes. When we reached the top we were so high up over the trees that the yachts on Lake Annecy looked to be no bigger than our thumbnails.

Keyna and I did not speak French but Susan and Bob did and they explained to us what was involved. At the launching area there was a little wooden ramp which ran out over the treetops at an angle of about 45°. The idea was that when you and Dominique, the guide, were strapped to the glider you ran in tandem down this ramp and jumped out over the tree tops into the wild blue yonder, with nothing but a small sheet of multicoloured canvas to save you from an early exit to eternity. Susan was game and she jumped, and in due course she arrived back, flushed and excited. Bob had been vomiting in the interim but now he was 'good to go' and he also returned from the experience intact and happy.

Now it was my turn. My heart was in my mouth as Dominique applied a belt around the two of us, instructed me to wrap my arms around his waist and signalled that we should run in tandem down the ramp and then jump. I was terrified that I would trip on the way down but we ran in harmony and jumped off the mountaintop. It was both an exhilarating and frightening experience.

Lake Annecy is now in view – 'NEVER AGAIN'.

We flew like birds in the sky, soaring up and down as Dominique tweaked the canopy this way and that. I can remember that, as we were getting closer to the lake and were seeking a safe landing area, I realised that I had not enquired what the drill was for landing. *'Dominique'*, I asked, *'what do you want me to do so that we land safely together'*? He did not, of course, speak any English! However, he was a skilful fellow and brought us both safely back to ground. I thought to myself, *'I'm not doing this again'!*

So we drove back up to the top of the mountain to pick up the others and return home. Keyna had originally made it perfectly clear that there was no way she was going to jump off any mountain. But when we got to the top we were all full of congratulations for each other, and when Dominique indicated that he had time for one more jump he pointed a finger at Keyna. Amazingly, she said yes and off she went. I have it all on film and showed it at her 60th birthday party, many years later.

On my return to IIB the question for me was how to capitalise on our new-found strength and market respectability. I promoted the bank in every way possible. I attended business functions, I became involved with the Irish Management Institute (IMI) and the Confederation of Irish Industry (CII) and together with my colleagues we did more than our share of entertaining potential clients. I felt we had a really good nucleus for the top management team in Ted, John, Pat, Liam and, more recently, Ronnie Fitzell and Brian MacManus who had joined us from Ulster Investment Bank.

*Left to Right: **Patrick A. Larragy**, Secretary and Corporate Finance Manager, **Edward A. Marah**, Banking Director, **Cornil Withofs**, Director, Treasury, Foreign Exchange, Marketing, **John A. Kelly**, Manager, Treasury, Foreign Exchange, Marketing.*

Members of IIB's management team.

*L-R: **Patrick A. Larragy**, Secretary and Corporate Finance Manager, **Edward A. Marah**, Banking Director, **Cornil Withofs**, Director, Treasury, Foreign Exchange, Marketing, **John A. Kelly**, Manager, Treasury, Foreign Exchange, Marketing*

We were, however, still very small in banking terms and growing the company through annual profitability was likely to take a very long time. We needed a more aggressive strategy. We had started our company and had gone a long way towards putting structures and an operational philosophy in place. One important area that was missing until KB's arrival was an appropriate remuneration policy for the senior group; now we were able to fill this gap. The philosophy was to pay salaries at no more than average levels but to

154

put in place a bonus scheme which would act as an incentive for management to buy into the company's medium-term strategy and targets. The key here was that the bonuses could only be earned after five-years had elapsed.

In October 1978, I wrote a document entitled *A Strategic Vision for IIB Bank*, which attempted to spell out a medium-term plan for the bank. It turned out to be weirdly prescient. The focus was to be on emphasising fee earnings and taking advantage of the strengths

Board of Directors of IIB Bank, from left Cornil Withofs, René Peuskens, David Kingston, Louis Delmotte, Ted Marah, Paul Vergote, Pat Larragy, Donal McAleese, Paddy McEvoy and Rony Van Hoeck.

of our two shareholders in international banking and Irish retail activity respectively. I presented this paper to our board and subsequently to the executive committee of KB, it was enthusiastically received. Our bank had been started at 'the worst of times'; there were energy crises, the collapse of the secondary banking market in the UK, and a world on the cusp of global recession. The energy crises of the 1970s were to provoke a new economic crux in Ireland which would endure throughout the 1980s. From the beginning, ill-considered efforts were made to re-activate the economy through spending programmes.

This resulted in massive levels of public debt and had a disastrous effect on economic performance throughout the 1980s. Successive governments continued the borrowing spree and income taxes rose to marginal levels of up to 60 per cent. Unemployment levels also rose. Not surprisingly this cocktail of high taxes and high unemployment resulted in a significant increase in emigration, with up to 40,000 leaving the country each year throughout the decade. The 1970s and 1980s were bleak economic times and certainly not hospitable for the banking industry. Our response was to be fast on our feet, and to be proactive and innovative in what was then a very sleepy domestic banking industry. We were always trying new things; many of them did not work but enough of them did. We pioneered creative ways to reduce the cost of borrowing for the Irish multinationals, and in 1987 we were the first bank to establish in the newly created Dublin International Financial Services Centre, Albert Reynolds, who was then Minister for Finance, was so impressed with our fast response to this government initiative that he invited me to his office for a photo-call. We arranged the first international syndicate for an Irish corporation (GPA Group) and the first privatisation of an Irish semi-state company (Irish

Continental Line), we arranged Irish Pound Bond Issues in Europe and we pioneered new money market products for the Irish corporate treasurer.

GPA signs $65 million loan.

Irish Intercontinental Bank in conjunction with its Belgium parent, Kredietbank N.V. has arranged a medium term $65 million credit facility for GPA Group Limited. The multi-currency revolving loan and guarantee facility is being lead managed by the two banks with IIB acting as Agent bank. Pictured at the signing in Antwerp were: Mr. A. Grupping, Managing Director, Kredietbank; Mr. Maurice Foley, President, GPA Group; Mr. Edward Wauters, Managing Director, Kredietbank; Mr. John Tierney, Chief Financial Officer, GPA Group and Mr. Paddy McEvoy, Chief Executive, IIB.

And in 1978 IIB established a joint venture with Irish Life which was to become Ireland's first centralised mortgage lender. There were some failures along the way, one of which turned out to be quite fortunate. After considerable research into the value of farming assets, the prospects for farm incomes under European Community membership, the relatively under-geared position of the farming community and the strategic importance of agriculture for Ireland we made a decision to enter the market for secured lending to farmers. We mounted quite a sophisticated marketing plan focusing on the county agriculture offices, local accountants and solicitors and other intermediaries. However, despite our best efforts the campaign was a resounding failure. As Ted recounted, *'We succeeded in getting four customers all of whom were delighted to borrow money from us but none of whom had any apparent intention to repay'*! Not wanting to throw good money after bad, we closed down that project.

KB took shareholder responsibility for IIB. From the very outset they gave us an unusual level of autonomy in the areas of staffing, in product development and in the setting-up of reporting and control systems. They did reserve the right to approve loans over a certain level, but the delegations to local management were generous. In effect, the running of the bank was under our control; the Irish Life shareholder commented how unusual this was but did not seek to change anything. I was conscious of the need to preserve this unusual degree of shareholder trust and I took pains to ensure complete transparency in reporting 'good or bad'. Louis Delmotte was KB's senior representative on our board; he and I hit it off from the beginning. Sometimes during my visits to Brussels I would stay at his home. He was one of the most exceptional men I have met; wise, courageous and always looking at the big picture. Many years later, when KB was experiencing serious difficulties in the international markets, they turned to him to take on the role of CEO and sort out the problems, which he did.

Louis Delmotte.

The work ethic and the sharing of a common philosophy among the senior group in those early days was the best I have ever known, it was a privilege to have been a part of it. The emphasis was on integrity, on innovation and on commitment to the customer; these were hallmarks of our institution. There was a truthfulness about the way we did business and an emphasis on knowledge sharing as we sought to educate each other. Our philosophy was that responsibility and authority were to be delegated as far as possible but always with backing and involvement from senior management whether things went right or wrong. Mistakes and failure were regarded as learning experiences. As a colleague said, *'Reporting of reality; that was encouraged, there was no fear'*.

Perhaps the most important ingredient was the culture of experimentation which permeated the entire organisation. I had acquired a lovely beachfront property in North Wexford and from the very early 1980s we would meet there towards the end of the year to review departmental plans. The directors would each present draft ideas based on discussions within their departments. Nothing was considered to be too far-fetched and every idea was given a hearing. Of course, most of the ideas were unceremoniously thrown out but those that remained became part of the annual corporate plan for the coming year. These plans were sacrosanct, until they were changed! After a strenuous day's work we would repair to the local pub for pints and then back home, to await the arrival of Mrs Keating from the Anchor Bar with a delectable evening meal.

David Kingston, the Irish Life CEO and IIB board member, used to tell me that I was *'a control freak'*. Perhaps, but I was a good delegator. There is a clear difference between delegation and neglect, and I would have been very conscious during my time as CEO that at the end of the day I was ultimately responsible for what happened. Working with Ronnie Fitzell, the Chief Financial Officer, I put a very heavy emphasis on back-office control systems. Many of the systems we put in place in those early days were ahead of their time, and KB was quick to acknowledge this, implementing some of them in their own operations.

160

My leadership style was definitely a collaborative one. The emphasis was on getting real commitment from colleagues to the extent that I would have preferred to achieve three-quarters of what I wanted and a real 'buy in' rather than 100 per cent and some resistance. If something went wrong I wanted to be given the opportunity to help in sorting out the problem, and if something went right I was very keen to see that the credit was apportioned down the line. One of my colleagues said, *'Paddy was able to stand back quite a bit. He never ran any department. He simply got you in and said, 'Now let's talk about that. What are you doing'? And then there was a list of eight or ten points'*.

For me, the personnel function is a line management responsibility and all that was needed was a personnel services function. So, right up until my retirement from the executive role I resisted establishing a human resources department in the normally accepted sense. In due course the bank did reach a size where this philosophy was no longer sustainable and a fully-fledged personnel department was then established.

There were essentially three initiatives that were responsible for the Bank's success: preference share lending, relationship banking and a revolutionary approach to mortgage lending in the Irish market

In 1979, we had an enormous piece of good fortune when we pioneered a lending product which had the effect of significantly reducing the interest cost for major Irish exporting companies. Nowadays the avoidance of tax is looked upon with suspicion and distrust; this was not the case in the 1980s. Because of the recessionary environment and high levels of inflation, interest rates were exceptionally high and this was frustrating the efforts of the IDA in attracting multinational companies to Ireland. The availability of lower cost finance was a huge boost to their efforts. It was promoted in their marketing literature, and they regularly introduced potential borrowers to us. IIB came to be known as the principal provider of this so-called Preference Share Finance (PSF). Our involvement was well known. On one occasion I had a call from the Finance Minister, Albert Reynolds, encouraging us to provide an unusually large facility to the General Electric Company of America. Conceptually similar schemes were in operation in other jurisdictions, for example in Belgium with its 'Coordination Centres', a fact known to the Irish Department of Finance.

As often happens, the pioneering of a new product is the brainchild of one or a small number of people; in this case it was one man, Pat Larragy. Pat always maintained that his initial motivation came from Donal McAleese suggesting to him that he should examine the Belgian/Irish tax treaty to see what opportunities it afforded. Pat worked on this idea for about a year and though I was keen to see him spend more time on traditional corporate finance activities, we had about 12 active clients in those days, he was resolute and he kept at it. He says himself that the key ingredient of this new product came to him when he was looking out at the sea, contemplating nothing in particular. The scheme was complicated but was based on the fact that the Irish government applied no tax on profits from exports. If a bank could stand in the shoes of an Irish exporting company it would enjoy this tax relief. The way to do this was to invest in the exporting company by way of a special class of preference shares. A limiting factor would be the size of the bank's own capital resources and in IIB's case we had little or no capital funds available. What Pat discovered was that through the Belgian/Irish tax treaty it was possible to create a lending product where the provider was a Belgian bank, for example KB.

The initiative nearly died at birth. Our first tax-based lending facility was to be the provision of a £12 million loan to a major Irish exporter in the dairy industry. This was a very attractive proposition for the borrower; and for us as, apart from a good return, the lending would be on KB's balance sheet and so would not use our capital funds. I had cleared everything with KB before the start of the board meeting which had been called to approve the loan formally.

I was both stunned and troubled when the KB representatives told us that they had had a change of heart and were no longer willing to become involved. We had put a huge amount of work into developing this scheme and we were satisfied that we had the necessary taxation advice. We had kept KB informed at all stages and we had taken every possible precaution to ensure that the documentation would stand up. The problem was that at the last moment, and despite previous agreement, some in Brussels were having cold feet about the idea. Since we had already made an offer to the exporter, there were reputation issues for us. I also felt it was a test of the integrity of our relationship with KB. I made it quite clear at the board meeting that the client had already been advised of a positive credit approval at all levels and that I was unwilling to go back to them with a change of heart. Louis Delmotte supported my position and after frantic phone calls between Dublin and Brussels the original loan approval was eventually re-confirmed.

We followed our philosophy of selling at reasonable prices and did not take advantage of the dominant position we had in the provision of this low-cost facility. Instead, we sought to take a fair and equitable approach in sharing the tax benefits with our customers. This special type of lending was likely to have a limited life so we sought to develop sustainable business relationships in other fields for the future. Our approach and philosophy was to build long-term relationships and encourage our clients to give us business opportunities in other areas.

IIB had an enviable reputation for business lunches in those days and we always saw 'having a good dining room' as an important part of our marketing drive. In the early days Johnny Steineger combined his responsibilities for driving and acting as general factotum with working as our *maître d'* and chef. I was very fond of Johnny and he was always looking out for my best interests. Among other things he was a *pâtisserie* chef of some distinction so it was natural that we would look to him for help with our lunches. He is remembered for a particular incident. Our lunch guest on this occasion was a Vice President with Marine Midland Bank, Nancy

Young. At the end of a splendid meal, Johnny came back into the dining room and, having changed into his *maître d'* uniform, asked Ms. Young,

'How would you like your coffee, Ma'am'?

'I like my coffee like I like my men, strong and sweet' she simpered.

'Black or white, Ma'am'? blandly continued Johnny.

One of the problems arising from our success was that we were always running out of space. Ultimately, we had to leave Merrion Square and move to dedicated new premises in Sandwith Street. Subsidiary companies were placed in other locations. However, in the early years we loved Merrion Square and felt that the address enhanced the presentation we wished to make to our customers. It happened that one of our directors had heard through a contact that the building to the right of our bank might be for sale. There was no prospect of us acquiring the building on the other side, it was too close to government buildings and there were would be security issues. The premises we were interested in was then used by the Land Commission, if 'used' is the correct terminology, since this agency of government had been moribund for quite some years. I can't recall how we managed to take a look inside but we did and, as we anticipated, the building would have been perfect for our purposes. It was Dickensian inside, with a small number of elderly people sitting on high stools, leisurely reading newspapers or writing up ledgers; there was an atmosphere of dust and decay all around.

I decided to call on Mr. Scully, then the Secretary General of the Office of Public Works. He was intrigued by my visit but perked up when I told him that we wished to acquire the Land Commission building. *'How much are you offering'*? He asked. *'I thought £250,000 would be a fair price'*, I replied. *'That seems a fair price to me'*, he responded, *'but the Minister for Finance, as you know, is resigning on Friday to make way for his successor and he will have to authorise any sale. I'm not sure this will be possible, but let me see'.*

The next day John Bruton, the retiring Minister for Finance, signed a document authorising the sale of what was the Irish Land Commission building to IIB, I understood it was his last official act. We subsequently heard that negotiations with the trade union representing the civil servants about their re-location were fraught. The issue had to do with the new bus routes, which were deemed to be inferior.

By the mid 1980's the bank had grown considerably. We had now reconfigured our premises to include a much improved dining facility and we had retained the services of Patrick Guilbaud, whose restaurant subsequently was awarded a Michelin Star, to provide lunches several days a week. However, the bank did not always shine. I recall an occasion when we had as our luncheon guest Noel Griffin, CEO of Waterford Glass, one of our most important clients. At the end of the lunch Noel asked me about the bank's view on the prospects for the dollar in the currency markets. I said to him, *'Let me have our Head of Treasury, Cornil Withofs, join us and he can give you an up-to-date view on this'*. When Cornil joined us I posed the question to him. He looked Noel Griffin in the eye and said solemnly, *'The dollar? It could go up, it could go down'*. That, I'm afraid, was it. I was less than pleased about this and when our guest left I went straightaway to Cornil's office and said something on the lines of *'I don't think you covered the bank with glory in your analysis of the prospects for the dollar; and, if you want to be technical, I would suggest that you left one of the options out, namely, that the dollar might stay as it was'*.

In due course nominal interest rates did decline and preference share lending lost its appeal. Largely through the goodwill gained by the relationships established we were now very successful in developing import/export, foreign exchange, term lending and deposit business with many internationally focused companies. This relationship banking with the corporate sector contributed significantly to our annual profits in years to come. The skills developed in the preference share lending era, including documentation, financial engineering, and credit analysis, translated well into this new approach. As banking director, Ted Marah deserves great credit for this success. Ted was exceptional in every facet of his role, and he was particularly influential in managing IIB's credit risk. He and I had a very close working relationship; indeed, colleagues used to say that we could read each other's minds.

The key to sustaining success in banking is the avoidance of bad debts. Overall we were very successful here but I can recall a few loans which caused us some anxiety. We were the first lending bank to GPA, which was on its way to becoming the most successful aircraft leasing company in the world. The original facility was guaranteed by the American bank, Continental Bank, which put it in a blue-chip credit category, and accordingly we decided that the right interest rate for this term facility should be 1¼ per cent (over our cost of funds). I was invited to lunch at the renowned Guinea Pig restaurant by GPA's founder, the redoubtable Tony Ryan. After the usual pleasantries, Tony told me that the rate of interest was to be 1 per cent. He told me that GPA was going to be a major international leasing company, that there would be very significant business for IIB with GPA in future years, but that the rate of the current facility was to be 1 per cent. He suggested that, if this was not the case, we could not expect further business with his company. I told him the rate was still 1¼ per cent and so it remained. We continued to operate as one of GPA's principal bankers over the years to follow.

In 1990, GPA placed a $17 billion order for 700 new aircraft over the following decade. These contingent liabilities were to cause the company's subsequent undoing. The decision to float GPA on the stock market in 1992 was unsuccessful, partly because of an aviation industry downturn following the 1991 Gulf War. The failure to raise the new equity capital was a disaster for the company. It now had $10 billion in debts. IIB had a significant, mainly bank-guaranteed credit exposure to the company at that time. In the end GPA avoided default on its debts by packaging and selling some of its aircraft to the leasing subsidiary of the General Electric Co., and used the cash from this transaction to repay its debt.

A second such transaction was potentially much more serious for us, in fact at one time it threatened to do lasting damage to the bank and its prospects. One day in the mid-1980s, the managing partner of one of Dublin's leading law firms introduced us to a potential business client. This was one, Dr. Ramos (not his real name for reasons of confidentiality) supposedly a Paraguayan national with vast experience in the international rape-seed oil business. In checking out Ramos's credentials, one of the things we relied on was a credit report from a well-respected Swiss bank which stated that, '*He is good for in excess of $10 million*'. The idea was that Ramos was to source plant from a leading and highly reputable company, which I will call International, and he was to take responsibility for commissioning and building a rape-seed oil manufacturing facility in Ireland. Initially, we turned down the transaction, but it emerged that there was also an offer of advisory business for us and on that basis the loan was approved by our and KB's credit committees.

The requested facility was in two parts, with the first relating to the purchase of the plant equipment to be provided by International for about $5 million, and the second being a facility of an additional $5 million to Ramos for commissioning the plant. Initially, these two facilities were to be separate, and were to be provided by way of letter of credit. With great good sense and foresight, the banking

169

department drafted a further document linking the two and stating that the end result would be International delivering a commissioned plant which would do what it was supposed to do. We insisted on a legal opinion from their internal counsel confirming that the three documents would achieve this.

Initially, everything went well; the plant was delivered from International and was available for the construction of the manufacturing facility. And then; nothing happened. All monies were at this stage committed and drawn under the letter of credit facilities but the plant lay fallow in the Dublin docks and Ramos had disappeared off the radar. This was worrying. The amount involved was the equivalent of a significant proportion of the bank's capital funds at the time. Approaches were made to the Paraguayan embassy in London, who had never heard of Dr. Ramos.

I genuinely feared that this event could profoundly damage much of what we had worked for. I could clearly see possible loss/reputation damage/fraught relations with our shareholders, and more. Eventually, we took the decision to allege fraud against International and their internal counsel. They took the view that they were only responsible for that portion of the letter of credit which related to the equipment which had already been provided by them. They informed us that they had assigned the contract back to Ramos and that we should pursue him on the matter. Around this time, we made contact with the CEO in the relevant subsidiary company of International and (amazingly) he disclosed that they had dealt with Ramos before and that, *'They knew what they were doing'*. He confirmed that he was aware that the linking of the contracts had been signed by the chief legal counsel of International but he nonetheless persisted in his view that the matter was now Ramos' responsibility.

We knew that legal action against International would be expensive given the likely long and costly court proceedings. I contacted Luc Wauters, KB's chairman, and suggested that he try to arrange a meeting in Brussels with the chairman and the CEO of International. This meeting was arranged in Brussels and attended by International's chairman and a senior Vice President together with Louis Delmotte, Ted, and myself. International, although a major player in the global markets only had a brass plate presence in Ireland with no assets, and we were aware that suing them in Ireland might not achieve anything.

Initially they continued with their position that the linking of the two contracts did not achieve the effect of making them responsible for the full loan. Our best hope now was that we could persuade them of the prospect for serious damage to the reputation of their company. In the course of these very difficult discussions we made them aware of our conversation with their senior colleague in the subsidiary company (I suspect they believed we had taped this conversation). A conversation in German ensued between the International representatives; a conversation which took place in the full hearing of our side. Whether this was meant to be confidential or not, Louis Delmotte understood German, and he called us aside and told us that they were now minded to settle the debt. After further protracted discussions and negotiation, they agreed to pay us back all but £120,000 of the amount due to us. When I got back to Dublin I had misgivings about the settlement and contacted the senior executive of International to say that we wanted all the money back. He was furious; he contacted Delmotte, who called me, *'Paddy, you can't do this, you have to compromise'*, the Belgians were great for compromising, *'We have to leave them with something'*. Eventually, and reluctantly I agreed.

Subsequently, we spent £35,000 in employing a detective agency to track down Ramos. When he was found he had multiple passports in his possession. He was now exposed as an international conman of Indian origin. He had only one unencumbered asset in his ownership, which was a substantial property in Knightsbridge where he lived with two young ladies. He was sentenced to a term of imprisonment at Reading Gaol. The judge allowed the monies we had expended on the recruitment of the private detective agency as a preferred debt, so we were paid back £35,000 from the sale of his Knightsbridge property. In due course, the BBC ran a programme on Ramos's world-wide fraudulent operations. We had not been the only targets, others being in countries such as Australia, Fiji, and Wales.

Chapter 8

IIB and How We Built a Bank
Part 2

Sports people talk about having 'momentum', when everything seems to go right for the player. Well, we had momentum back in those days. It was like collectively being in the zone.

In 1987 the Irish Government decided to establish the International Financial Services Centre (IFSC) in the Dublin Docklands. This initiative was designed to attract major international banking and financial operations to Ireland, primarily by offering generous taxation and other incentives. The plan had been mooted for some time and when it happened we were ready to move. As mentioned earlier, we were the first banking operation to be granted a banking licence in the new centre.

Our 'Docks' company (KBCFI) was a joint-venture with KB, profits being shared between us. The company began with the equivalent of £100 million of equity capital, initially concentrating on financing the international aerospace sector, where the early experience with the GPA group allowed us to become the market leader in the provision of aerospace services. In his 1987 Chairman's statement, Donal McAleese said the bank was fully supportive of the concept underlying the IFSC. He added: *'The Government's commitment to the progress of this project is clear and we are impressed by the practical and supportive approach taken by the Department of Finance and by the IDA in the discussions leading up to the approval of the licence'.*

KBCFI was a wholly-owned subsidiary of KB, but was run and managed by IIB. I acted as company Chairman and Liam Donlon, Ted's deputy in the banking department, was appointed as its General Manager. Liam was a member of a talented family, his brother Seán had been an influential Irish ambassador to the United States and his sister Regina was head of the Loreto nuns in Ireland. Our success in building a significant and profitable internationally-focused project management business was principally due to the talent and dedication of Liam Donlon. He has sadly passed on now. I remember him as a friend and as the best and most sophisticated dealmaker I have encountered. Project finance is a complicated and risk-laden business. The rewards are significant and appropriately so given the challenges involved in structuring, negotiating and documenting the transactions. We had an outstanding executive team under Liam's direction and when KB eventually took the decision to phase out this activity the senior people were much sought-after by other international banks and project finance companies.

By 1989, the trust reposed in us by our Belgian owner reached a whole new level when their executive committee decided to transfer all of their international project finance to KBCFI, together with responsibility for its future development. Over the coming years KBCFI established offices in the UK, in New York, and in Hong Kong, and by 2005 would become a multi-billion dollar business with a reputation for leading project finance syndicates in aerospace, energy, telecommunications, transportation, and shipping.

Our strategic plan also called for us to work in partnership with our minority shareholder, Irish Life. The CEO of Irish Life and their representative on our board, David Kingston, and I were friends. Our business relationship was based on trust and it was because of this trust that Irish Life, who were at the time one of Ireland's premier financial institutions, controlling more than 50 per cent of the domestic insurance market, agreed to a joint venture with us in setting up a revolutionary new mortgage company in Ireland. This was the first specialist mortgage company of its kind, sourcing business through Irish Life's broker connections. We had been looking for ways to work with Irish Life in the retail sector. Initially we made numerous efforts to develop a retail banking presence in Ireland and in the UK by way of acquisitions but all of these were

With my friend and colleague, David Kingston.

either outright failures or insufficiently profitable to keep our attention.

The main problem was that the philosophy and approach underlying retail banking was very different to that in corporate and investment banking. Corporate banking was natural for us but retail banking was another world. There was also the question of access to customers; competitor banks with their branch banking systems had a natural distribution system for retail products. But we had no intention of replicating this costly way of doing business.

Our initial forays into retail banking included leasing, consumer finance, and hire purchase. We bought small companies but we were always tentative. Yet we knew that to be successful in these areas scale was essential. Recognising the need to have a completely different mindset in approaching retail banking we eventually decided to move a small cohort of people to different premises and tasked them to come up with ideas. Brian MacManus was put in charge of this initiative.

Brian was a gifted and creative marketing man and a passionate supporter of the bank's philosophy of customer orientation. He bravely took on the harder challenges, notably the attempt to develop a retail business in the UK. This attempt to establish a mortgage banking business in the UK, in collaboration with Irish Life, was not a success, though we learned a great deal from the experience.

We recognised from the start that there were only four requirements for the setting up of a centralised mortgage business:

namely, product, distribution, processing and funding. To fulfill these needs, the Irish Life brokerage system was to be our customer procurement arm, we copied existing mortgage product from the UK market, we outsourced the processing of business to the Trustee Savings Bank (TSB), and the funding was to come from KB. The business plan envisaged the first-ever 'virtual' bank; in theory a really low-cost operation. It worked in theory but I'm afraid not in practice. The problem was the low quality of the business which we generated; effectively we had allowed the Irish Life brokers to do the mortgage underwriting, the idea being that we would do a post sign-off review. But by then of course the money was gone out the door.

This was a salutary experience for us and we were never to repeat the error. Perhaps the most important thing we learned in this UK venture was the application of technology to processing. We subsequently bought state-of-the-art software and adapted it to the Irish market, where we were market leaders for the next five years in terms of processing.

The Irish Homeloans initiative was established as a 50-50 joint venture between IIB and Irish Life but the staff was mainly drawn from our side and I was appointed as Chairman, board meetings took place in the elegant surroundings of Irish Life's corporate headquarters. Brian Duncan, the General Manager at Irish Life responsible for their broker relationships, made it quite clear that they had no interest in embarking on this project unless they could target 20 per cent of the mortgage market. That was fine with us.

There was standing room only at the first meeting to introduce this new concept to the Irish brokerage market; the attendees were very enthusiastic.

We laid down a set of clear criteria for customers, such as steady employment, an earnings multiple and so on. This was in the relatively early days of bank lending on mortgages, and borrowers of other banks at the time were never told the criteria by which the loan applications were judged. Mortgage approval carried with it an

178

air of grace and favour and mystery. The open, straightforward Homeloans initiative was both daring and new and the result was that on the first week of opening we were swamped with applications for mortgages. Ted recalled, *'We had so many applications coming in that the directors would take home bundles in the evening'*.

To slow down the flood of applications, we had to increase the required earnings multiple, understandably this was not well received by our Irish Life partner at the time. But we still had an attractive product and it caught the attention of the public. First-time mortgage applicants now had a simplified mortgage system to deal with, they only had to fill out a single application form and they would get a decision within 24 hours.

When the Irish mortgage lending initiative was established, Brian MacManus was the obvious man to manage it. Initially, his challenge was to educate the Irish insurance brokerage community in the intricacies of mortgage lending. As a first step, he prepared a document aimed at the brokers which he called *The Business Builder*. This document set out in great detail a marketing programme to help the brokers both to develop business and to understand mortgage lending. It contained flyers, brochures, and posters for customisation by individual brokers and even an audiotape which could be used on local radio. Homeloans grew in strength and reputation from the outset and was constantly bringing new and imaginative products to the market.

A meeting I had in 1989 was to come back to haunt me. Richard Fenhalls, the first secretary of our bank, introduced to me to Des Traynor. Although I had never met him before I was aware of his prestigious standing in the business community, as the chairman of both Guinness & Mahon Bank (G & M) and CRH Ltd. When we met in my office he advised me that he was in a position to place significant deposits with us, he explained that they now needed another banking institution as they had reached the limit of what was appropriate for them to place with G & M. I introduced him to a colleague from the deposit section. The deposits in question grew to a substantial size and it subsequently transpired that they were part of the famous Ansbacher deposits, which were held as part of a tax evasion scheme on behalf of hundreds of individuals, some of whom were household names in Irish business and professional circles. Many years later IIB was alleged to have been complicit in this fraudulent tax evasion scheme. It took a great deal of time and effort by the management to respond to these allegations, and although the bank continued to grow strongly, inevitably there was a real cost to us in terms of the opportunity cost of that time. We had built up an enviable reputation over the years and no stone was left unturned by the senior management in their efforts to preserve this. After various tribunals and other forms of enquiry the bank was fully exonerated from any wrongdoing.

By the early 1990s, business volumes and profitability had grown rapidly making a constant need to build our deposit base. IIB was always funded partly from money market sources, along with commercial and private deposits. This was not a problem, given our strong credit standing, or so we thought. IBCA, the international credit rating agency, had awarded us a rating of A1 for short-term and A+ for long-term credit, which now put the bank on a par with the country's top two Associated Banks. However, a storm was brewing. By 1992, unprecedented volatility in exchange and interest rate markets precipitated a currency crisis in Europe. The exchange rate mechanism suffered a terminal blow on 15 September, 1992, otherwise known as 'Black Wednesday', when sterling devalued. Mortgage rates in Ireland were now ranging between 12 and 14 per cent and trending higher. All of this precipitated a major crisis for Homeloans, which significantly relied on short-term wholesale funding rather than more durable customer deposits. The company had to raise mortgage rates twice in 1992 from 14.75 per cent to 17.75 per cent, at a time when our competitors were keeping their mortgage lending rates at significantly lower levels.

At one point, attempts by the authorities to protect the Irish currency from being devalued sent short-term interest rates as high as 100 per cent. Lending at 18 per cent and borrowing at 100 per cent simply could not be continued. We could not allow a subsidiary company to bring down the bank, which is what would have been in prospect if we were to continue subsidising the full mortgage book at the levels required. On the other hand, if we passed on this extra margin cost to mortgage customers it would, without doubt, have led to the demise of the mortgage company as our customers fled to other institutions.

I had a major row with the Central Bank at the time. I took the view that, since we were perfectly capable of funding our mortgage book in any currency apart from the Irish pound, it was their responsibility to ensure that we could access the money markets for Irish pounds at reasonable rates. I got nowhere. I decided to make contact with someone who, I felt, would know the Irish Government's position on devaluation. He took my call and, while he was not specific, he did say something along the lines of, *'Paddy, if I were you, I think I would wait for a couple more days'*. This we did, and within those couple of days the Irish pound devalued and the markets stabilised. Despite this hiatus, the upward momentum of the bank's profitability continued that year and thankfully our mortgage customers stayed with us.

One of the really important things KB did was to help us in establishing a top-class foreign exchange and money market operation in Dublin. They nominated one of their senior men, Cornil Withofs, to take charge of this, and to be their local board level representative at IIB. Cornil was the first of the senior group to reach retirement age, and following on his retirement, John Kelly, who had been with the bank before I joined, took over. John was a particularly creative man who left a significant legacy of innovation in the Dublin foreign exchange and money markets. What I remember most, though, was his famous 'School for Yuppies'. Foreign exchange and money market dealers were scarce and expensive and it was difficult to distinguish the difference between good and not so good ones. A similar problem had arisen for the availability of fighter pilots in the Second World War when the solution was the creation of aptitude tests which looked for the required skills. So John teamed up with Pat Shortt of ETC Consult in Dublin to build a series of tests that would improve our chance of selecting successful dealers. We piloted the tests by trying them out on our own dealers.

Having acquired a team of new trainee dealers the next challenge was to give them the required experience without exposing the bank's money. So we built a simulated trading room with all the things a real trading room would have except it was not trading real money. We had phones, telexes, admin systems, risk monitoring systems, news and market feeds and more. We also had trainees join us from the Central Bank, Irish Life and KB. One of the main reasons it worked, which we did not anticipate, was that the trading in the dealing school became just as challenging as the real thing. It made the *RTÉ 9 O'Clock News* with Bryan Dobson (who still remembers it), and it migrated to KB in Brussels later.

By 1989 effective economic policy changes were finally implemented, including the prohibition of borrowing to finance certain categories of current spending. A deal was struck with the trade unions who agreed not to take strike action in return for gradual, negotiated pay increases. Crucially, Fine Gael undertook not to oppose the necessary government economic measures in an agreement known as *'The Tallaght Strategy'*. Following on these measures the Irish economy returned to growth in the 1990s, although unemployment remained high for a period of time. This was to be the beginning of the Celtic Tiger years, when by the year 2000 we would become one of the world's wealthier nations (or at least we thought we were), with unemployment at 4 per cent and income tax at almost half the levels prevailing during the 1980s. The economy grew by between 5 per cent and 6 per cent for a number of years leading to dramatically rising standards of living and in due course surpassing many of those in Western Europe. In 1999 Ireland joined the euro currency system along with eleven other European Union nations.

IIB having survived and indeed prospered during the difficult economic circumstances of the 1970s and 1980s was now faced with the new challenge of operating in a growing economy. Work continued at a frenetic pace for me, and trying to find the balance between work and leisure was always an issue. In a very real sense my work was also my hobby and I found it difficult to turn off from work issues outside so-called working hours, whatever they were! Keyna always insisted that we take real family holidays and we did, and on occasion the two of us managed to get away on our own. I never had difficulty in delegating and always had total confidence that Ted and the senior management group would keep me informed and would call me for my views (or decision) when necessary.

Islands have always held a particular fascination for me. Before journeying to Boston and the Harvard Business School we spent two weeks on the largest of the Aran Islands to reconnect with our roots before this great adventure. Sometimes, before my annual holiday I needed to spend a couple of days on my own on one of the beautiful islands that dot the Irish coastline. Clare Island was special but by far my favourite was the lovely island of Inishbofin, just 10 km off the North Connemara coast and a 30-minute crossing from the fishing village of Cleggan. The tranquillity and beauty of this place would overwhelm me; beautiful sandy beaches, at least one pub as I remember (which never closed), and solitude.

Seamus Heaney's poem, *Seeing Things* captures the memory of the crossing and anticipation for me:

> *'Inishbofin on a Sunday morning.*
> *Sunlight, turfsmoke, seagulls, boatslip, diesel.*
> *One by one we were being handed down*
> *Into a boat that dipped and shilly-shallied*
> *Scaresomely every time. We sat tight*
> *On short cross-benches, in nervous twos and threes,*
> *Obedient, newly close, nobody speaking*
> *Except the boatmen, as the gunwales sank*
> *And seemed they might ship water any minute'.*

Keyna and I had always wanted to visit South Africa but, along with many others, we would not go there so long as the policy of apartheid persisted. When it finally came to an end in the early 1990s the two of us set off for an extended holiday to that great country. The early part of our holiday was in Cape Town, with visits to Table Mountain, the beaches and the wine region. We hired a car and journeyed down the fabled Garden Route intending to go all the way to Durban. By Holy Thursday we got as far as

Plettenberg Bay and were stunned by the beauty of the local scenery and its extravagant beaches. We decided we should stay there for a week or so. We had made no reservation and so, with total confidence, I sought out the local real estate agents to see what options we had for a rental.

The news was not good. Nothing was available, it seemed. By 4.30 in the afternoon, and knowing that the real estate agencies would be closing by 5 o'clock we still had nowhere to stay. We were very conscious that the Easter holiday period was now upon us. We tried one more rental agency and again no luck. I was in big trouble at this stage (for my usual deliberate lack of planning on holidays) and as we trudged wearily out of what was probably the last agency in town the lady from the agency ran after us saying, '*I do have one place available, it's the architect's property with six bedrooms but it is very, very expensive*'.

'*Very expensive*' is a relative term; she initially quoted us £150 for the week and we negotiated this down to £100, a great bargain for us. She told us that she would arrange some home help and that a young black girl would be coming in the morning. She told us what the going rate was for this work (a pittance) and instructed us not to exceed the going rate on any account.

We slept late the next morning and when we finally came out of our front door we encountered a young lady sitting on the steps with a canvas sack on her back and a baby in tow. She said that she had been waiting for an hour but did not feel it was her place to ring the bell. Princess was her name and she turned out to be a very efficient and likeable young lady. Later when Keyna asked what she would like as a gift, she replied, '*A suitcase, please. I have nowhere to put my belongings*'.

So, Keyna took her to a local department store where they purchased one of the best suitcases (with a lock) in the shop. We broke the rules and gave her much more than the going rate, plus numerous gifts of food and clothes for her and her family.

On the local golf course we met a man and his teenage son; the man had only one arm and he played golf off an 11 handicap! South Africans had been starved for company from overseas visitors during the apartheid years and they seemed very happy to make our acquaintance. We were asked to join them at their house for a dinner party. Throughout the party the men sat on one side and the women on the other side; the men talked local politics and local sport and Keyna tells me the women talked only about family and shopping. Discussions about cultural matters or world affairs were not possible and the issue of race relations was a no-go area. They were doing their best but it was a nervous evening for all.

Going public

I had developed a reputation for speaking out on economic issues of national importance. The high profile enjoyed by the bank because of our growing market share and profitability, together with the stream of new initiatives we introduced, meant that I received a certain amount of attention from the financial press. I was from time to time featured on the cover of popular financial journals such as

Irish Business or *Business & Finance*, occasionally chosen as *Man of the Week* and once *Irish Banker of the Year*.

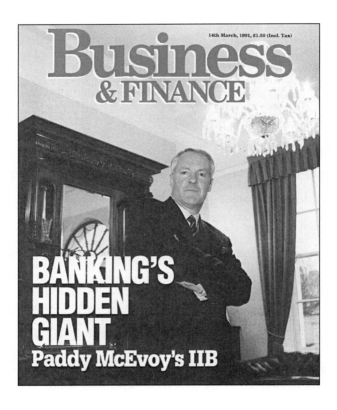

The press we got was invariably positive and in one of the business magazines we were ranked in the top six banks in the country for growth in assets, third in assets per employee, fourth in percentage growth in shareholders' funds, and ranked as number one in the categories of annual growth in after-tax profits and return on shareholders' equity. KB was delighted with this sort of publicity which they saw as being far more important than I did. It was a disappointment for them when my enthusiasm did not match theirs.

In my years at IIB, I felt strongly that I had a responsibility to participate in the business community organisations of the day, seeing this as good for the image of the bank. I took a keen interest in the activities of the Irish Bankers' Federation (IBF) and was elected as its President in 1994. Although IIB's clientele was essentially the larger Irish companies I now had the opportunity to endorse the IBF's position in regard to the environment for small and medium-sized enterprises.

Joint effort could boost small firms

THE PRESIDENT of the Irish Bankers Federation has called on the Government and the banks to get together in an effort to tap the potential of the small business sector.

Speaking at the agm of the IBF yesterday, out-going president Mr Patrick McEvoy said that the banks had a vested interest in the vigorous and long-term development of the SME sector — even though the experience of lending to small firms during the recession has been poor.

The IBF is looking for the implementation of a loan guarantee scheme along the lines of that operated in Britain, where the government gave £155m worth of guarantees to small and medium-sized enterprises last year.

Mr McEvoy said a similar scheme here would allow companies with good ideas, but no track record, easier access to finance at reasonable rates.

The IBF chief also wants greater co-operation from the small business sector, particularly when it comes to sharing financial information.

Mr McEvoy said the banks would not be found wanting when it came to developing initiatives to help small firms. Finance Minister Mr Ruairi Quinn had asked the banks to develop such initiatives when he scrapped the bank levy.

■ Patrick McEvoy . . . the banks have a vested interest in the long term development of the small firms sector.

The Small Firms Association (SFA) had been particularly vocal in the previous year on the issue of lack of government initiatives and on what they viewed as insufficient funding and unattractive rates from the banking sector. I met with Lorraine Sweeney, President of the SFA during my year and we agreed an approach, including measures which, following consultation with the other banks, could now be endorsed by the IBF. At the 21st Annual Conference in 1995 when keynote speeches were made by Bertie Ahern, Minister for Finance and Maurice O'Connell, Governor of the Central Bank, I was able to say that the IBF was collaborating with the SFA to lobby government for equal treatment for the sector, and for amendments in relation to the law on preferential treatment from the Revenue Commissioners. I was also able to say that IBF had lobbied successfully for the introduction of a loan guarantee scheme.

By far my most important business involvement was with the Confederation of Irish Industries (CII); I served on the executive committee for many years with about fifteen others, all industry leaders in their fields. I was the only banker on the executive committee and as such felt I could bring a unique point of view to the table. I formed a close relationship with Liam Connellan, the very able executive director of the CII and his redoubtable colleague Con Power, the director of economic policy. My most important role within CII was chairing the economic and taxation policy sub-committee. One of the functions of this sub-committee was to make the annual pre-budget submission to the Minister of Finance of the day. Bertie Ahern TD was Finance Minister at the time, and I can recall one meeting when our subcommittee, together with the President of the CII, Paddy Wright, Michael Smurfit's right-hand man, had a notable success in persuading the minister to make important adjustments to the tax code for Irish business.

A Confederation of Irish Industry meeting with Minister for Finance, Bertie Ahern TD on our budget submission. Picture includes David Croughan, CII economist on the left and Tom Jago, President of the CII on the right.

It was not my first contact with Bertie Ahern. This happened when I was chairing a committee to raise funds for Dublin's oldest youth club, the Belvedere Youth Club. One of our fundraising targets was the Arthur Guinness Company, and we were hoping that they might be persuaded to give us a donation of £25,000. We met for lunch with a main board director Tony Prendergast, a past Belvederian, and I remember Tony telling us that it was unlikely that their MD would give us this amount of money. However, on the way out of the lunch he said to me, *'There is one way you might get money from him. We are having major union problems at the moment and it might help if the Minister for Labour, Bertie Ahern, was to write to him and ask for it'.*

Nothing daunted, I attempted to ring the Minister for Labour and surprisingly got him on the line. I explained the situation to him, knowing that the youth club was in his constituency, and his response was immediate, *'Okay'* he said, *'why don't you send me a draft of the letter you would like me to send to the Guinness company'*. I sent him a draft letter, he liked it and Arthur Guinness & Co. gave us £25,000 for the youth club. There was no publicity in this for Bertie Ahern; I think he behaved wonderfully.

By the mid-1990s, the bank was flying high; market reputation, profitability, and return on shareholders' equity were at record levels, and I was a happy man. One day I left the bank at lunchtime and walked around the corner to Nassau Street, past the Oriel Gallery. I vividly remembered how its owner, Oliver Nulty, had sold me a beautiful George Russell (AE) painting entitled *Sea Spirit*. When I took off the wrapping at the back of the painting I discovered to my delight that the provenance of the painting noted that it was a gift from the artist to Lily, sister of W. B. Yeats.

In my reverie, I was tapped on the shoulder by a man whose face was vaguely familiar. He said, *'Are you Paddy McEvoy, you must remember me'*? I had to admit that I did not, and he reminded me that we were both young men in Ballymote back in the early 1960s. *'There is something I really want to tell you'* he said. *'You may recall that the two of us were trying to date the beautiful Olive Egan in those days. Well, one night I was at the local cinema and to my deep annoyance you and she were sitting together a couple of rows in front of me, and you did something which I have never forgotten,*

192

you produced a box of Cadbury's Milk Tray, I realised then that I was out of my league'.

We had a good laugh about this and other reminiscences. Later on, I got to thinking and realised that in a certain sense the wheel had turned full circle, from Ballymote to now. I began to start thinking that maybe I should move on, that I had given my best to the bank, and that there was an obvious successor in Ted Marah and a top-class senior management team in place. The thinking process took root, and I decided to resign the CEO role. The shareholders asked me to stay on as Chairman (Donal was keen to retire at this stage), and I was more than happy to do this as long as my work commitment was very significantly reduced. I got some commentary in the financial press and the usual *'leaving to pursue other interests'*. Frankly, I had no idea what these were going to be.

From the very beginning, Hannah Crowley was my secretary and PA. Throughout all these years she was much more, she was my friend and regularly my counsellor. The bank had ticked so many boxes for me in terms of my social philosophy and my senior colleagues were also my friends.

When I resigned from the CEO role a number of events were held in my honour, including a staff reception and a function for our customers at Trinity College. The latter event gave us a real opportunity to make a statement about what IIB stood for in front of a gathering that was representative of Ireland's leading companies and top decision-makers. The function was attended by over four hundred people, including business leaders, colleagues, family and friends.

In my address I expressed my gratitude to so many different people and along with Ted I talked about the ethos which the bank aspired to and I finished by quoting Hemingway, '*The first and final thing you have to do in this world is to last in it and not be smashed by it; and that is the same with your work. This is both a rule for the conduct of life and a rule for the conduct of art; to last and to do work that will last*'.

Digression on capitalism

I have always been focused on the long-term approach. The good side of capitalism is that it has proven itself as an unparalleled mechanism for improving efficiency and creating jobs in the process of building wealth. However, today the system is seriously criticised and held accountable for a whole range of economic, environmental, and social problems. Increasing global wealth inequality is being laid at the door of the free market system and the legitimacy of business is being questioned. The Nobel economic laureate, Milton Friedman has been the market system's great champion, preaching that business fulfills its social responsibility simply by pursuing wealth creation. From the time I first started thinking about this issue (back in my Harvard days) I have been in serious disagreement with this point of view. Writing for the *New York Times Magazine* in 1970 about *The Social Responsibility of Business,* Friedman said, '*I have been impressed time and again by the schizophrenic character of many businessmen. They are capable of being extremely farsighted on matters that are internal to their businesses. They are incredibly shortsighted and muddled-headed on matters that are outside of business but affect the possible survival of business in general'.*

His argument that every business should pursue profits only (and thus fulfill its social responsibility) has always been qualified; he also says in his iconic book *Capitalism and Freedom* that business should pursue profits *'So long as it stays within the rules of the game, that is to say, engages in open and free competition without deception or fraud'.* Abuse of market power and manipulation of the rules of competition seem to me like good examples of 'deception or fraud'.

I have a more fundamental disagreement with the view that conducting business as usual adequately fulfills a company's responsibility to the community and to society. Increasingly, enlightened companies and researchers on business school campuses (mainly in the United States) are redefining capitalism along principles of shared value, which involves creating economic value in a way that also creates value for society. This is not philanthropy but a different approach to achieving economic success. It is not necessarily about personal values and it is not a re-distribution approach; the underlying idea is to increase the long-term pool of both economic and social value. This seems to me an approach which is both ethical and principled.

Postscript

Despite being part of the process or maybe because of it, I was always trying to get a better understanding of the cultural factors which can lead to innovation, market flexibility and renewal. Many years later, after I had resigned from the chairmanship of IIB, I entered the Ph.D. programme at UCD to investigate this phenomenon of strategic renewal and I used our experience at the bank for the study. The study was a qualitative one, relying on archival material, extensive semi-structured interviews with IIB managers and established theory. In order to reduce the potential for bias my thesis supervisor required that I exclude myself from the list of interviewees and from attending any sessions with former colleagues. Accordingly, I arranged for colleagues from the Ph.D. programme to conduct interviews with effectively all of both the first and second-line managers who had been with IIB from 1973 until 2005.

The evidence supported the theory that continuous strategic renewal is associated with the type of institutional values that prospered in IIB in those days; those of disciplined ambition, trust and support, and most importantly a willingness to experiment. There was virtual unanimity among interviewees (including those who had retired) in relation to these values. In particular, the culture of experimentation was to the forefront. I examined the archives in relation to the annual corporate plans and the number of attempted new initiatives ran into the hundreds, the majority of them failing but some succeeding spectacularly.

It is important to create an environment and an atmosphere where the generation of ideas is encouraged and where creativity is applauded; there is a need to step back and make room for other people to flourish. The important thing is to build a sense of community where people can join together in a shared sense of purpose. The building of trust is entrepreneurial gold. Trust can take a long time to gain real traction but it can be lost in a heartbeat. And above all trust is about ethical behaviour, transparency and respect for others.

Chapter 9

Chairman Years

When I resigned as CEO in 1995 I had no idea what I was going to do next. But being only 56 years old there was, I felt, a nice balance between experience and energy. Recollections of the bank years filled me with joy and continue to do so to this day.

I never had any regrets about my decision, I just felt that my race had been run as CEO and it was time to move on. I did however feel somewhat proprietorial about IIB and I was happy to stay on as Chairman. Modern corporate governance thinking is against a retiring CEO taking on the chairmanship role. Former CEOs can dominate the board agenda and decisions and make it difficult to discuss steps that may reverse a course of action identified with the former regime. Alternatively, a sensitive former CEO may be unable to contribute constructively to board discussions without being concerned that he/she will undercut the effectiveness of their successor. An example justifying modern thinking on this would be the case of Anglo Irish Bank where the CEO moved up to the chair on retirement. This is generally agreed to have been a significant contributor to the subsequent debacle. Seán Fitzpatrick hung on to the chairman's role, offering the explanation that the new CEO, David Drumm, was young and needed mentoring; the Regulator was powerless to do anything about it. The orthodox viewpoint was eventually adopted by KB, and they were right to come to this conclusion

As the dominant shareholder, KB made it clear that they wanted me to stay on as a quasi-executive Chairman for a period of two years. The idea was that I was to have a continuing input on strategic development, while Ted would be responsible for the executive management of the company. This was a silly idea which only worked because of the special relationship which Ted and I had. But it was a challenge for the two of us; for me the challenge was to move out and to leave the stage to my successor and for Ted the challenge was to adopt the mindset appropriate to that of the chief executive. I never had any doubt in my mind that if we had a serious disagreement I was the one who had to go and I said so at the time.

Nineteen-ninety-eight was a special year for us, marking 25 years of the bank's history. We had a great story to tell and to mark this special anniversary we organised a celebratory party for those who had been part of the journey with us. I had prevailed on the Taoiseach, Bertie Ahern TD, to make the keynote speech. Dismayingly, two days before the event I had a telephone call from Celia Larkin on behalf of the Taoiseach to inform me that unfortunately he would not be able to attend because the Clintons, Bill was President of the US at the time, had made a late decision to come to Ireland and he needed to be available for their visit. I was devastated by this news and said so. An alternative proposal offered to us was that another government minister would attend in the

Taoiseach's place and would speak at the event, this minister had a reputation for trenchantly criticising the banking industry and I made it clear that while we would be happy to welcome her we would not be calling on her to speak. *'Let me talk to Bertie again and I will come back to you'* Celia replied.

Later on that day she called me again and told me that the Taoiseach would attend and would speak, and he would then journey by helicopter to Limerick to greet the Clintons. Bertie did attend and he did speak, he stayed with us for several hours; and he added hugely to the success of the occasion. We were very grateful to him.

A Czech interlude

Towards the end of 1995 I received an approach on behalf of the International Monetary Fund (IMF) inviting me to participate in a team which was to visit the Czech Central Bank (CCB) with a view to advising them on the privatisation of the banking system. The initial contact came from Brian Wilson who was then working as a Vice President with the World Bank, since his retirement from AIB Brian had joined the World Bank as a consultant and was now reporting to its President on change management issues. My initial reaction was that I knew little or nothing about the banking system in Central and Eastern European countries and even less about the privatisation programmes which followed the end of the communist era. Brian encouraged me not to let my lack of experience deter me, pointing out that I could expect to be with others on this mission who would have all the necessary experience.

My next contact was from Elizabeth Milne at the IMF who also assured me that other team members would indeed be in a position to speak to all of the issues that the Czech authorities had identified. In particular, M. Gilles Denoyal, director in charge of privatisation for the French Ministry of Economy and Finance, was to be part of our small group and we would also be assisted by an experienced government representative from Germany. Ms. Milne identified the topics to be discussed with Governor Josef Tosovsky of the CCB as including:

- The appropriate speed of privatisation
- The appropriate role for government ownership, if any
- Monetary risks that might emerge as these large banks were privatised
- Whether the bank's loan portfolio should be cleared of non-performing assets prior to privatisation and, if so, how
- The appropriateness of the takeover of small weak private banks by large banks prior to privatisation
- The role of the Central Bank, if any, in the privatisation process, and
- Legal aspects of privatisation.

At this stage of my life I was a fairly confident man but this agenda was daunting. I was given a host of documents germane to the issues to be discussed by the IMF and the World Bank and I spent a considerable amount of time preparing for this visit. In the IMF's final communication with me it was explained that the privatisation process was already underway. They had started the partial privatisation of a number of the larger banks by way of a 'Voucher Privatisation system' by which the public at large were offered ownership in the banking system through the issue of vouchers at minimal or no cost. I was also given an itinerary of the visit, which was to last for three working days. I was checked into the Intercontinental Hotel, and given best wishes for the mission's success.

On Sunday 30 November on arrival at my hotel in Prague there were two email messages waiting for me. The first was to inform me that M. Gilles Denoyal, the French expert on privatisation, would not be joining us, *'due to unforeseen circumstances'* and the second was to inform me that the expected member from Germany would also not be arriving, once again *'due to unforeseen circumstances'*.

I was alarmed by this. My understanding was that the Czech Central Bank was looking for expert advice in the area of privatisation, and while I had some book learning on the topic I had absolutely no experience to call on. I felt that I had made my position perfectly clear in the first instance to Brian Wilson and subsequently to the IMF. Now another email arrived advising me that, *'We have now informed the Czech Central Bank that you will be heading the mission and will be on your own; in accordance with the agreed itinerary they will be expecting you at 9 am tomorrow morning Monday'*.

I slept very badly that night, being kept awake by scenarios of what might happen. The following morning I ventured to the CCB's headquarters, a nondescript grey building on the outskirts of Prague. My first meeting was to be with Governor Tosovsky. I understood this to be of an introductory nature following which I would spend briefing time with his colleagues at the Central Bank over the coming two days, the intention being that I would lunch with the Governor on the final day to give him *'conclusions and expert advice'*.

Governor Tosovsky received me very cordially; he made it clear that there would be no limitation on the provision of information to me, and that if I wished to interview additional people at the Central Bank or at the Department of Finance that could be arranged. He asked about my background from both a business and academic standpoint. Being Irish was a huge plus. My briefing notes had told me that Governor Tosovsky was highly respected by all parties within the Czech political system both as an economist and as a banker, and that he was also well regarded by foreign investors. He had the reputation of being a non-confrontational person but with the ability to persuade his opponents to accept his views. My initial impression of him was very favourable, and despite my concerns about my lack of experience confidence began to grow. In particular, my banking experience was going to be valuable, and my philosophy of adherence to high prudential standards had struck the right chord.

I spent the next couple of days interviewing the senior people at the CCB on their experience of privatisation and on their approach to the next phase. Incredibly, I was finding that the material was all familiar to me. The quality of new bank ownership was going to be key in terms of a capacity to bring capital and expertise but more importantly to sustain standards of governance, independently of the requirements of the local regulator. The Czech banking system had only recently emerged from the centralised state-owned structures operating in the socialist and communist era and it became clear to me that there were significant legacy issues in relation to the quality of the loan books and the corrupt practices that would have been a feature of the past.

As planned, I met again with Governor Tosovsky over lunch on the Wednesday. It was a one-on-one meeting over three hours. I was very familiar with the territory at this stage and I outlined to him the highlights of what would be contained in my written report. In particular I stressed the importance of 'cleaning up' the Czech banks' loan portfolios in advance of privatisation, and strongly recommended that they ensure that new owners were in a position to bring capital, expertise and high standards of governance.

He was quite forthcoming on the legacy of corruption and I recall him talking about the existence of mafia types who were going to be very resistant to any plans for 'cleaning up' the banks. He told me that he had personally received death threats and needed the protection of a bodyguard. Before I left he expressed an interest in my continuing in a consultative role with them for the privatisation programme, subject to funding coming from the World Bank or the IMF.

I completed my report within a week of my return, copying it to Governor Tosovsky and to the IMF. Shortly afterwards Elizabeth Milne from the IMF responded very positively saying, *'The Czech authorities have indicated to me that they found your visit to be particularly useful at this formative stage of thinking on the subject of further privatisation'*.

She indicated strong support from the IMF for a continuing consultancy assignment with the Czech authorities, pointing out that this would be appropriately part of the remit of the World Bank. Unfortunately, as it transpired, the World Bank had only recently closed down their office in Prague and they had no interest in supporting the project financially. This was the end of my involvement with the Czech banking system

Postscript

After the disappointing results of the voucher privatisation scheme the Czech authorities did start looking for strategic investors for the four large state-owned commercial banks. The first of these was the Republic's third largest commercial bank. Unfortunately the new owner saw itself as a portfolio holder rather than a strategic investor, hoping to sell on at a profit in the short-term. There was a run on the bank deposits and the closure of the bank in June 2000.

The problems were partly inherited since the balance sheet and loan portfolio were not dealt with prior to privatisation. The Czech Central Bank acted swiftly and decisively, selling the institution to a rival Czech commercial bank within two days of the bankruptcy.

Hungary

The Czech interlude was only a teaser and around this time, the end of 1995, I was contacted by both David Kingston from Irish Life and Remi Vermerin, then in charge of international activities for KB, to inform me that they had acquired a minority equity participation in one of Hungary's largest banks, Kereskedelmi es Hitelbank (K&H), in partnership with the European Bank for Reconstruction and Development (EBRD) and the Hungarian State. Following the tender process KB and Irish Life had acquired a joint 46 per cent ownership in K&H, with the balance being shared between the EBRD and the Hungarian government. Although KB's shareholding was as low as 23 per cent it fell to them as the bank investor to play the key role in staffing and corporate governance. David Kingston and Remi Vermerin asked would I have an interest in acting as chairman of this bank for the initial three years following privatisation. I had no hesitation in saying yes.

While our experiences at IIB had given me the highest regard for KB and its senior management I was to come to the conclusion that they can be faulted for their shareholder contributions to K&H. The due diligence was seriously lacking in terms of assessing the quality of the loans being acquired and even more importantly the quality

206

of K&H's management team. KB's lack of experience in international banking soon became evident. It would have been normal for the principal bank shareholder to safeguard their own and the other shareholders' interests by placing some of their personnel into key management positions; the reality was that KB simply did not have such personnel available to them in these vital early years.

I had for long been fascinated with Hungary. For the past thousand years its history had been full of great events, battles, kings, allies, intrigue and enemies and occasionally peaceful years. In the 13th century the Mongols invaded the country and half of the population (one million people) were killed or deported as slaves; it was overrun by the Turks in the 16th century; and then it became a Hapsburg dominion. Hungary was allied with Germany and Austria in the First World War and then with Germany against Russia in the Second World War. After the Second World War it was under the dominion of the Soviet Union for 44 years and in 1989 finally achieved the status of an independent democracy. I was to find the Hungarian people to be profoundly doleful and have often wondered whether their history and legacy of defeat in battles and wars were contributory factors.

K&H was established by the Hungarian State and inherited banking responsibility in the areas of agriculture, the food industry, commerce and tourism. Following a domestic merger in 1996 the bank now qualified as a Universal Large Bank boasting the second-largest branch network in Hungary. As the first step in bank privatisation in 1997 the EBRD provided significant loans, in order to strengthen the bank's capital position. From the outset it was intended that my role would be a non-executive one. It was represented to me that the loan book was sound, that the bank was very well capitalised and that the management team under the direction of Janos Eros was first class.

Board meetings were originally intended to be on a monthly basis but in the event my presence in Budapest was required much more often than that. Initially this was because of my requirement for acclimatisation but as time moved on it became increasingly necessary to deal with emerging problems. Irish Life's first nominee to the board was its chief executive, David Kingston, while the KB nominees were from a lower management level. The board also included two nominees from the EBRD, and three members of the management team. I felt that the experience I had just had with the Czech Central Bank would be very valuable and I expected similar issues in relation to non-performing loans, limitations of the management team and legacy corruption issues. I still retained the chairmanship of IIB but looked forward to this new role as the beginning of a great adventure. It was, but not quite as I expected.

The first event was the signing of both the share purchase agreement and the shareholders' agreement in July 1997. I was informed that the Finance Minister, Peter Medgyssey, was prepared to interrupt his holidays for the signing of these documents. An international press conference had been convened together with a host of receptions and what was described as *'a prestigious walking dinner'*.

I was met at Budapest International airport by a representative from K&H, whisked through all the airport formalities and driven by limousine to the bank's headquarters. The driver, Gabor, told me that his instructions were that he and the limousine would be available to me throughout all my future visits to the bank. Unfortunately, all of my luggage had been mislaid by the airline, including the suit which I intended to wear to the various meetings and functions. Panic stations Hungarian style followed. Being Sunday evening the men's clothes shops were closed at this time and special arrangements had to be made for a prestigious man's shop to open up early on Monday morning. I acquired a new suit, shirt, shoes (they never fitted properly) and a splendid new green tie. When I finally arrived at the bank on Monday morning the shareholder meetings were in progress and I was ushered to the top table which looked down on a very large gathering, including several television crews.

At the completion of the shareholder business everyone stood up and we all shook hands with one another. I then met the CEO Janos Eros. The bank premises were spectacular but the CEO's office was even more splendid. Janos Eros was small, in his early 30s, and it would be an understatement to describe him as fat; flesh simply wobbled on him like jelly. He subsequently told me that in his youth he had been a member of the Hungarian fencing team, not like this, I thought. He was on his feet to greet me warmly when I entered his office. He expressed his great pleasure at the outcome of the privatisation negotiations, he promised ongoing commitment to the bank (and to me!). He asked me if I had any questions. I don't recall what my question was but I do recall that he said, *'The President of our country would be the best person to answer that, let me ask him'*. He then picked up the phone, made a call (all in Hungarian and presumably to the President) and acquainted me with whatever new knowledge he had received. This was quite intimidating and perhaps intended to be.

I spent the next couple of weeks in Budapest, meeting with my colleagues at the bank, with the local shareholder representatives and with senior government officials, all part of an acclimatisation process. Our first board meeting took place at the end of these two weeks. It was high farce from start to finish. The boardroom at K&H was magnificent, with a huge polished oak table with floral displays in the centre and the walls adorned with an impressive art collection. I discovered that it was the practice to invite others to attend on the understanding that they did not have speaking rights. Headphones were provided for each of the participants at the meeting. A glass booth was in one of the corners occupied by two young ladies, both of whom had their headphones on. I realised that the proceedings were to be multilingual (Hungarian and English) with simultaneous translations provided. There was a massive agenda and a stack of papers about a foot high relating to these agenda items. The majority of these papers had been given to me and to the other new directors, immediately before the board meeting. Janos was deeply apologetic about this and assured me that it would not happen again. At the start of the meeting there were lengthy introductions of all those attending. This took about an hour.

Each of the agenda items was presented by one of the executive directors reading from a very detailed prepared script. I had never seen anything like it; it just droned on and on. Understandably, the new board members asked many questions and the responses went on interminably. We were learning nothing, nothing about the loan book, nothing about the evolution of liquidity and capital ratios, nothing about the issues that were facing the management, and nothing about the relationship between the bank and the regulatory authorities. The whole thing lasted for more than four hours, followed by a sit-down lunch which, at least, was superlative as far as the cuisine went. It was, in fact, a world class 'snow job', far surpassing anything I had ever seen in Ireland.

Before returning home I met Janos in his office and told him what I thought. I told him that I was used to board meetings focusing on the real issues and I expected the business of our board to be concluded within a couple of hours. I also told him that the external board members expected to have all of the papers delivered to them several days before the meeting, unless there was some exceptional item which had only come to light in the few days preceding. I told him there was to be no more simultaneous translation and that all meetings were to be conducted in English. I told him that attendance at the board meeting was in future to be restricted to board members only. Finally, I told him that he and I were to have a pre-board meeting to discuss the items arising and to agree how they might be handled. His response was to say that these were all great ideas and they would be implemented immediately.

It became the practice to circulate (most of) the board papers to directors about a week before the upcoming board meeting. This gave me the opportunity to phone Janos to discuss whatever was on my mind. There was no direct flight from Dublin and it was my habit to travel from Dublin to Frankfurt and then onwards to Budapest, this took about eight hours but was the fastest and most reliable route. The bank had arranged for me to stay at the five-star Kempinski Hotel while the other visiting board members were housed at the less grand Intercontinental Hotel. From the beginning I was conscious of the preference shown towards me, and was concerned about being compromised. I concluded that this was the way things were done in Hungary. I usually arrived at my hotel at about 10 o'clock on a Sunday night, ushered through airport security by a K&H representative and driven by Gabor in the limousine provided. Inevitably (despite my pleas) there was a significant amount of additional paperwork to be reviewed in advance of the next day's meeting. Board meetings were always scheduled to start at 8 o'clock and it was my practice to go to the Intercontinental Hotel for a 6.30 am meeting with my colleagues from KB/Irish Life and the EBRD. These meetings were absolutely vital, giving us an opportunity to decide what we wanted to achieve at the board meeting and how we would go about it. We were like-minded in our intent to have productive and information-laden meetings and to ensure that the shareholder requirements were fully understood. This schedule gave me very little time for sleep and despite the occasional use of sleeping tablets I was usually operating on adrenaline the following day.

The arrangements I had with the shareholders allowed me to bring Keyna with me several times a year and on those occasions we would stay longer in the beautiful city of Budapest. Janos Eros made herculean efforts to win my goodwill; there was nothing they would not do for me or for the two of us when Keyna was with me. On one occasion arrangements were made for us to tour the premier art galleries, accompanied by an art expert, at a time when they were normally closed to the public. On another occasion the Houses of Parliament were opened specially for us and again a tour guide was arranged for these magnificent buildings which were built in the style of those at Westminster. Keyna's recollections are interesting:

'We were treated like royalty. Usually about a week before my visit, I would receive a request asking what I would like to do during my visit, together with some suggestions and the amount of time that might be allowed for a particular activity. A car would meet us at the airport and we were whisked through customs and immigration as VIPs. The driver would take us to our hotel and give Paddy his bundle of papers and tell him what time he would be collected in the morning. I

would then be advised of my itinerary for the following morning and a car and driver and tour guide would be at my disposal. I particularly remember how on one occasion I asked for a repeat visit to an art gallery and stating that this time I wanted to view the paintings on my own and would not need a guide. I subsequently found it quite embarrassing walking around the gallery with my driver several paces behind, following me around the gallery. It was quite difficult to concentrate on the paintings'!

The State Opera house in Budapest is one of the most beautiful in Europe and bears comparison with La Scala in Milan and the Paris Opera House. When I asked about going to the opera I was advised that this was no problem since the bank owned a box in the opera house. The opera house itself was extremely ornate in the baroque style with long flowing white marble staircases, rich furnishing, and high ornate ceilings, and with the walls decorated with wonderful frescoes of famous Hungarian artists. The stage was enormous and allowed room for all the great operas to be performed. Surprisingly, the price of tickets was very reasonable as it was part of the culture of Hungary that opera should be available to everyone. Our box was situated in a prime location in the opera house with a wonderful view of the stage and over many visits we saw operas and ballets including The Nutcracker, The Marriage of Figaro, and Swan Lake'.

Together with the other shareholder directors we were taken on boat trips on the Danube, and to the north of the country to see the famous equestrian shows. I particularly remember that, on 20 August 1998, to celebrate Hungarian Day we were all invited to join our Hungarian colleagues for a special entertainment on the riverboat *Rakocsi* to view a marvellous fireworks display and to listen to the music of Mozart and Mahler.

My responsibilities required me to be in Budapest for longer periods than the other shareholder directors. It was customary for me to stay for several days after the board to spend time with the CEO and his colleagues and to get a better understanding of the country and its people. K&H were very good about arranging for me to meet with some of the top people in the business and financial world, including the key state agencies and government departments. Dr. Josef Hajdu, who had public relations and protocol responsibilities in the bank, normally set up these meetings and attended them with me, I really enjoyed this type of thing; apart from introducing myself it was an opportunity to talk about our aspirations for the bank.

I was sometimes required to give interviews to financial journalists and to the daily press. These interviews were normally printed in full in Hungarian and could take up several pages of a particular journal. The Hungarian language, which is close to the Finnish language, is complicated and difficult to master. During my time I got to know a number of the diplomatic corps, many of whom had been there for several years and none of them, with the single exception of the Canadian Ambassador, who was legendary for this, had managed to learn Hungarian. I talked to Janos about this once and his response was, '*I don't understand what the problem is, here, our five-year-olds have no difficulty mastering the language*'.

The new shareholders had ambitious plans for K&H including the development of bank/assurance activities, providing state-of-the-art information technology, developing the international focus and generally playing a role in helping Hungary's progress towards membership of the European Union. In my days with IIB I had been convinced about the importance of developing trust within and outside the organisation, about the importance of having a philosophy of contribution to the community, and about operational integrity. At K&H I lost no opportunity to emphasise our intent to promote this philosophy. I'm afraid it was a lot more difficult than I expected and when I left several years later these aspirations would be at best a work in progress.

The Hungarian economy went through a bad patch during my term as chair of the bank. There was a sharp drop in aggregate demand leading to a decline in GDP. There were also internal issues which loomed large including the competence of the management team, cost overruns, legacy issues in relation to the quality of the loan book, and all this against the backdrop of possible corrupt practices which seemed to be endemic in Hungary. According to Transparency International's 2000 report *Corruption in Businesses*, top managers from Hungary's major companies said they regularly bribed politicians. The report claimed that *'Corruption is the standard and not the exception for most businesses; it is what defines success'*.

I made every effort to establish a good rapport with Janos. This was not difficult as I found him to be most agreeable and good company. He was a very intelligent man, with considerable gravitas. On one occasion he told me that he had been chosen as Hungary's *'Man of the Year'* in competition with the former King, a famous football star and a world renowned diva. When I asked him how he managed to achieve this he said with a big grin, *'I bought it'*. I did not know whether to believe him or not.

We socialised from time to time and he paid me the compliment of inviting me to dine at his home together with his wife Ursula. Looking back, I realise how difficult it would have been for him or anybody else who had come through the communist system to have embraced the management philosophy that I had in mind. His father had been Hungary's main man for overseas banking and finance and as such he and his family were automatic members of the elite. I soon found that he was on close personal terms not just with the state President but also with the leading politicians in both the main parties. When Janos walked the corridors of the bank junior staff literally stood against the wall as he walked by, and if he entered the lift the ordinary staff members would vacate it. He used to refer to them derogatorily as *'the brown suits'*. On one occasion my driver, Gabor, made a suggestion to me about an improvement in scheduling. When I told Janos about his idea he took it as a criticism and immediately wanted to dismiss him. '*Not on my watch, you won't*' I said. Gabor did remain at K&H throughout my chairmanship but when I tried to contact him after I returned home he had gone. He was a very talented man and I have little doubt that he would have been able to procure other, and probably better, employment.

Janos did not seem to have any interest in visiting the branches but I did. I suggested a joint outing for this purpose. He chose the town of Debrecen, which borders Rumania and the Ukraine. Next to Budapest, Debrecen on the east of the country, is Hungary's largest city with a population of about 200,000 and is one of the country's most important cultural and academic centres. During the Second World War Debrecen was almost completely destroyed, 70 per cent of the buildings suffered damage, and 50 per cent of them were left in rubble. After 1944 the reconstruction began and for a short time Debrecen became the capital of Hungary. The citizens began to rebuild the city, trying to restore its pre-war status, but the incoming communist government of Hungary had other plans and the institutions and estates of the city were taken into public ownership, with private property taken away.

The bank had several branches in the city and the hinterland. Agriculture was big in Hungary and K&H was the dominant bank for this sector. I don't remember the branch visits but I do recall that we were invited to visit the HQ of Hungary's principal agricultural institute, which was located within the city's university complex. The institute's premises was an impressive four-storey building and we were shown into a large conference room where about twenty members were seated in a large circle. I was put beside the Director General, with Janos on my right. The Director General stood up, said some really nice things about Janos and the bank and turning to me said, *'It is a pleasure to have you here Mr. Chairman. I wish to inform you that the last two speakers we had for this august body were the former German Chancellor Helmut Kohl and Mr. Gorbachev from Russia. Mr. Gorbachev was most disappointing but we really liked Herr Kohl's speech. What do you propose to speak to us about'*?

Again, the session was to be bilingual with translation services from Hungarian into English available. I had had no idea that I was going to be asked to speak. I said that I would like to speak about Ireland's position in the European Community and in particular the implications for agriculture. I said that I was aware that Hungary planned to join the European Community shortly and that my preference would be to make a very short address and answer their questions. This was easy territory for me and it worked quite well.

Occasionally I had the opportunity to meet with Hungarians who took the opportunity to criticise 'the system'. One of these was our tour guide for the visit to the art galleries. She had been educated in Moscow and was the holder of a Ph.D. in economics. She claimed that the management in all the banks was corrupt, and that corruption was the norm in the country. She gave the example of her mother who had a heart condition and needed to visit a heart specialist. It happened that the specialist she wished to attend was her first cousin, but even then she would not make the appointment until she had enough money to pay the obligatory 'gift/gratuity' to him, despite the fact that he was paid by the state and his services were supposed to be free to the public. This apparently was common practice in Hungary; a Gallup survey in 2000 found that 77 per cent of respondents thought it was 'typical' or 'highly typical' to give a gratuity or tip to hospital doctors, and more than half of the population believed that if they wanted proper service in a health care institution they had to pay.

On one of the occasions when Keyna was with me I mentioned to Janos that we would like to visit the Balaton Lake during our free time. The Balaton, the 'Hungarian Sea', is a 50-mile long lake with silky green-yellow water in the middle of the Transdanubia district. It is the largest lake in Central Europe and is one of Hungary's most precious treasures and most frequented resorts. Janos immediately set out to arrange our visit. It was about a three-hour drive from Budapest. When we arrived, chauffeured by Gabor, we were ushered to the quayside of the lake and introduced to the captain of a very large yacht which had apparently been assigned exclusively for our visit. We had no initial interest in going on a yachting trip so we went back to the hotel, intending to do some sightseeing. We spent the next day and a half exploring this beautiful territory and intermittently coming back to the hotel for meals and refreshments. What we did not realise was that the captain stayed on the quayside throughout the whole of our visit in expectation of our possible return and in the hope that he would be of service to us. I felt very uncomfortable about all of this, fearing that it went well beyond what might be described as normal hospitality.

At this stage KB were becoming concerned about the lack of profitability, the poor control of costs, and the competence of the CEO and his team. There were also concerns about some of the practices at the bank and some of the perks that were available to the senior management including recreation centres, opera boxes, hunting lodges, the Balaton yacht and the like. At my request KB sent in their internal audit team; their report was highly critical both of the transparency of reporting and of the performance of the management team. Janos was summoned to Brussels to a meeting with Herman Agneesans, the Executive Director of KB in charge of international activities and I attended. Herman criticised Janos severely on the quality of reporting, on the management of the loan book and on the control of costs. He made it quite clear that the shareholders would have to look for a new chief executive unless significant improvements took place. Janos was quite goodhearted about all of this, not overly defensive, and promised that the future would be *'as transparent as glass'*. When we met outside after the meeting he gave me the impression of being rather pleased with his performance. We parted on good terms and with renewed promises from him for the future.

The operational performance of the bank continued to decline, though it is important to note that this was in the context of declining GDP in Hungary. The extent to which the performance of the loan book was a legacy issue or could be attributed to the state of the economy was moot. What was important was the management of these assets, the controls on new lending and the control of costs generally. The board and the shareholders continued to have concerns and losses continued to mount.

Around this time I learned that there was an arrangement in place whereby senior bank staff and others associated with K&H could make investments, with the bank guaranteeing quite a spectacular rate of return. This was patently nonsense when stock market prices were in decline and the bank was losing money. When I was next in Brussels I shared these concerns with Remi Vermiren, who had now become CEO. KB was at this stage overstretched internationally and had no staff available to put into K&H so he asked me to be patient. I felt I had no option but to put my concerns in writing and this did get action but I felt very uncomfortable about putting Remi on the spot. It was now agreed that Janos Eros' services would be dispensed with immediately. KB identified a Czech national, Pavel Strnad, to act as interim CEO pending the recruitment of a long-term replacement. I was asked to look after all the necessary arrangements.

On my return to Budapest I made contact with Janos, who was travelling by car when I caught up with him. I told him that we had lost confidence in him and gave him the opportunity to resign, explaining that we would put a contract in place to deal with severance issues. He was remarkably calm about this, he thanked me for the opportunity given to him to resign his position and proposed an early meeting to discuss details. I engaged the best lawyer in Budapest's top law firm, subsequently I discovered that this gentleman was also advising Janos Eros; this, presumably, was a Hungarian version of a Chinese wall.

Shortly afterwards the interim CEO arrived and asked to be introduced to all of the senior management. I called a meeting for this purpose and even suggested to Janos Eros that he would attend this meeting and '*say the right things*'. He obliged, he attended the meeting, he facilitated introductions, he spoke well of the bank, he complimented me and he wished Pavel well. I was obliged to him and was happy to hear subsequently that his friends in high places had arranged for him to take over the CEO role in another state-owned banking institution.

Herman Agneesens and I were deputised to recruit a suitably competent new chief executive. With the help of an international recruitment agency we identified a list of three possible candidates and winnowed it down to one who seemed to be exceptionally well qualified. Tibor Rejto had strong academic qualifications and relevant banking experience with Citibank in Central Europe. His references were exemplary and we employed him. KB was now taking a much closer interest in the day-to-day affairs of the bank and was regularly using their internal audit team for this purpose. Tibor proved to be an excellent choice as CEO. He quickly put improved systems in place, he reduced the headcount and he slowed the pace of bank losses. He was very professional and I enjoyed working with him; in particular we worked well together in the management of the board agenda, and board documents were now arriving in a timely manner.

The EGM that nearly brought down K&H Bank,
Tibor Rejto on left of photo.

A crucial Extraordinary General Meeting, February 2000

My term was now coming to an end. However, losses at the bank over the previous few years had been at a level which led to a reduction in the share capital of the bank to the point where it was in breach of regulatory requirements. A somewhat complicated operation at an Extraordinary General Meeting was necessary to vote on the reduction in the bank's required level of capital, and then to approve a significant further injection of capital by KB in order to sustain operations in future years. Among other things this would represent a vote of confidence in the future of the company by the shareholders as well as a vote of confidence in the new CEO and his team. I had no idea that at this EGM issues were to arise that could well have brought about the demise of the bank.

In accordance with normal procedures the full board was in attendance as well as representatives of the State Privatisation and Asset Management Holding (APV), the agency which held the government's 32 per cent shareholding in the bank, together with legal counsel for all the other parties attending. As was the custom, the principal TV stations and the daily press were also in attendance.

I had been put on notice by Miklos Andrasi of APV that he wished to speak in advance of consideration of this matter. He addressed the meeting as follows: '*APV wishes to settle the matter of the capital structure of K&H by negotiation with the other shareholders and thereby ensure the future of the company to the satisfaction of all the owners. I am authorised to propose the adjournment of the extraordinary general meeting for a period of 30 days*'.

The other shareholders were not in agreement with this and the proposal was rejected by a margin of 2 to 1.

Tibor then made an excellent presentation in which he said: '*The year 1999 has seen a number of challenges for K&H. The new management has addressed three broad issues: Firstly, we redeveloped the way our group conducts its business and its business procedures and have involved our subsidiaries in this process. Secondly, we initiated a number of IT projects required for the efficient operation of the bank. Thirdly, we decreased and by the*

225

end of the year had reversed the unprofitable business activity of the bank'.

He noted that the required ratio of shareholder funds to total bank assets was 8 per cent under both the Hungarian accounting rules and international accounting standards. However, this ratio had now decreased to 5.11 per cent and this level was unacceptable to the banking regulator. He went on to point out that the bank had commissioned PricewaterhouseCooper to assist them in the determination of the appropriate rates and arrangements for the capital increase. He then recommended that the meeting approve the planned increase and restructuring in the bank's capital.

At this point Miklos Andrasi of APV indicated his desire to speak again. To the astonishment of all he said, *'Since the General Meeting was not suspended in accordance with our proposal . . . we must vote against the forthcoming agenda items. Thank you'.*

Although they only had 32 per cent shareholding in the bank this entitled them to a blocking majority in the context of the proposal before the meeting. I responded, *'Sorry, I have a question. Could you repeat your last sentence? Is it that because the meeting voted against your proposed suspension of the EGM, that you have a mandate from APV to vote against the capital increase proposal? Do I understand you correctly'?*

Andrasi confirmed that my understanding was indeed correct. I was really worried at this stage being conscious that if the proposal to increase the share capital was rejected it would be reported on national television that evening and in the newspapers the following day. The likely consequence of this would be a run on K&H's deposits with potentially disastrous implications for the bank, the shareholders and the management team. Playing for time, I again addressed the meeting, *'I have an important question. I would like to express myself very precisely. I think there are some contradictions in what you're saying. If I understand your words correctly, since the meeting voted against the suspension proposal, you argue that your hands are tied by APV and that you are mandated to vote 'No' with reference to the proposed capital increase'*? The answer to that question was again, *'Yes, we do and we will'*.

I had visions of disaster at this stage. At the back of my mind I suspected some Machiavellian plot to engineer the ownership of K&H back as a Hungarian state-owned institution. Back in my Bank of Ireland days I remember my old boss Jack Stanley used to say, *'There's nothing like the gallows to crystalise the mind'*. I think I did a smart thing at this stage, *'I will order a short break in order to have a consultation with all the shareholders. Ladies and gentlemen, I order a 10 minute break. Thank you'*.

The shareholder consultation actually took many hours and what were later described as *'strenuous and constructive'* negotiations between APV and KBC (KB), but at the end of it I was able to call on the KB representative who said, *'I can now make the following proposal on behalf of KBC Bank. We have noted the APV's expressed intention to vote against today's proposal for the capital increase; in the circumstances we now propose that KBC Bank will*

227

now formally propose an adjournment of this EGM to reconvene in March 2000, on the understanding that APV is now agreeable to consider such a capital increase.' KB had agreed to pay a significantly larger premium for the new shares and APV was willing to sell its shareholding on this basis. We had also been in contact with the Banking Regulator and I was in a position to say that they expected that the recapitalisation of K&H would be completed to their satisfaction. It was a great relief; I felt that a crisis had been averted.

The subsequent board meeting took place on March 2000 and the authorised representative of KB said that the parties had come to an agreement, subject to conditions. The June board meeting gave effect to the completion of these proposals. It was to be my last board meeting. Tibor and the executive management of the bank gave me a terrific sendoff, and a bound book detailing the highlights of my three years, including, the above verbatim transcript of the meetings and inscribed by all of the team, *'With our heartfelt thanks for all your help and assistance and advice at the helm of the Board of Directors of K&H Bank'.*

Privately Tibor thanked me for my handling of the EGM. He showed me press cuttings which confirmed my concerns. The financial press speculated that the state-owned OTP Bank (the largest Hungarian financial institution) was in the wings to acquire K&H, in the event that the EGM failed to resolve the capital increase issue. It had been quite a close call.

I did more interviews with the press; I said how much I loved Budapest, its wonderful architecture, the sense of history, the sense of culture, the opera house. I said I appreciated how well disposed Hungarian people were to Irish people; that we shared a lot in common, both being rural countries with dominant neighbors. And what was the 'lesson', the added value for me? *'The added value for me was the enormous satisfaction of being part of the continuing transformation and change process in Hungary in its movement towards the market system. This was a great privilege and a great honour and at the end of the day it reinforced for me the importance of the fundamental principles of honesty, integrity and thinking for the long-term'.*

And so I left Budapest and K&H Bank with fond memories of the country and its people and a determination to return again, as a tourist.

Some years later Remi Vermiren invited me to visit him in Brussels. On the flight out from Dublin the latest issue of the in-flight magazine had an article about Russian banking and Russian bankers—it quoted from a blog about mafia activities: *'Banking executives, reform-minded business leaders, even investigative journalists were systematically assassinated or kidnapped. In 1998 alone, members of the eight criminal gangs that control the Moscow underworld murdered 10 local bankers'.* When I got to Brussels Remi told me that KB was in the process of acquiring Absolut Bank in Russia and would I like to consider being chairman of this bank. I declined!

*Alan Dukes TD presenting the Irish Hungarian Economic
Association's annual award in 1998.*

My understanding and intent was that I would be a non-executive
Chairman of K&H and I was led to believe that the bank was in
excellent shape with a top-class management team at the helm. This
was far from reality and at times I did feel that my role became a
quasi-executive one, at least until the arrival of Tibor Rejto. The
problem for me was that I had deliberately resigned from the
executive function at IIB and I had other plans for the balance of
my life. Also, I was conflicted having regard to my responsibilities
as Chair of IIB and the increasing responsibilities I was taking on at
Belvedere College. I have always had a good capacity to

concentrate on the task of the moment but my experience is that there is a price to be paid for this level of application; I needed some downtime. Holidays have always helped in providing this balance and so did golf.

Chapter 10

The Pleasures of Golf

I have had some success at the game, winning Captain's Prizes at two prestigious golf clubs, Milltown and the European Golf Club, Brittas Bay, and succeeding in getting my handicap down to the respectable level of 13. Winning at Milltown is a special memory for me. I had only taken up the game a few years earlier and was now playing off 17. Effectively the full male membership of this famous club teed off in the Captain's (Paddy Dempsey) Prize. On the 18th I had a 5 foot putt left for a net score of 64, the ball did a lap of honour around the hole before finally dropping in. I felt I had a good chance of winning a prize with that score, but the problem was that I had not put my name down for the Captain's Dinner, which was now fully booked. I had only been a member for a year and election to this famous club was rightly considered quite an honour. I felt that to just turn up to receive a prize (any prize) would be looked on as discourteous. Shortly after I arrived home I got a telephone call from the Hon. Treasurer and my former classmate at Belvedere, Paddy Shorthall, '*Come on up here quickly, McEvoy*' he said, '*you are the winner of the Captain's Prize and you better be at the dinner, I have organised a place for you*'.

I would not have been a popular winner. The Captain's Prize was traditionally 'the major' of the year and the strong preference would have been that it was won by a long-standing member and not a newcomer. I made a decent acceptance speech that night and the party went on until the early hours of the morning. Paddy Dempsey's prize was a beautiful cut glass tankard with a silver top, suitably inscribed. I walked home that night clutching my boxed prize and I dropped it; miraculously, it remained in one piece. I remember coming home sheepishly at about 2.30 am and finding Keyna still sitting up waiting for me, together with her good friend, Mary Laffoy.

Not a big trophy but a big win for us at the K Club when John Bruton TD presented the annual Fine Gael golf trophy to our four-ball including Derry Egan, Paddy McEvoy, John McGilligan and Gerry Dempsey.

I only played in the big time once and that was when I was teamed with the famous Masters winner, Ian Woosnam, alongside Ian Curley, the chief finance officer of the Smurfit Company. The event was the Pro-Am which took place at the K Club before the start of the Irish Open. Our three-ball got fifth overall and would have done much better had it not been for Woosnam three putting the 17th. The dinner that night was in the elegant K Club dining room and I recall we were all kept waiting for an interminably long time for the arrival of the owner, Michael Smurfit. At one stage during the convivial pre-dinner drinks I bumped into the famous Northern Ireland comedian Frank Carson. *'What have you got to tell me'* he asked.

I remembered an anecdote I had heard about the American comedian, George Burns, and had the temerity to retell the story. It goes like this: Burns, who was at this time in his 93rd year used to say that the first thing he did every morning when he woke up was to call for the newspaper and review the obituary column. *'If I'm not in it, I get u*p' he would say. Carson laughed out loud and said, *'I'm due to roast John Mills tomorrow night and will use that story'*. *'You will, of course, credit me'* I said. He is still looking at me.

We sat beside 'Woosie' at the dinner that night, he is an unforgettable character and great company. My abiding memory was late in the night his explaining to Keyna the intricacies and importance of the correct arm rotation in the golf swing. Woosie was to finish second in the British Open that year. He lost by a shot having been fined two shots for having too many clubs in his bag.

This was the fault of his caddie, the same caddie who was on his bag during the Pro-Am at the K Club.

My great friend Noel Walsh would arrange golf outings with his medical consultant friends at his holiday home in Rosslare, where I was a frequent visitor.

Keyna and I with our friend Noel Walsh at his Rosslare home.

I was very fond of Noel; he was an unusual man, great intellectual company and generous to a fault. He was a great adventurer who practiced psychiatry in Canada, Ireland and Malaysia. Noel introduced me to the former President, Paddy Hillery. Paddy was to become a firm friend and golfing partner. For many years he and I used to play together against Noel and Jack Maloney. Over the years Paddy and his wife Maeve were guests in our Wexford holiday home and we stayed with them in their County Clare residence at Spanish Point. I felt privileged by his friendship, regarding him as an exceptional man who made a very real contribution to Irish society over his years as a government minister, European Commissioner and then for two terms as the President of our country. Despite his achievements he had a natural humility, a great capacity for fun and stories, and an enviable life philosophy. I remember one night in our Wexford home we were all discussing how we would confront death and he said when it came to him he would confront it like *'The Gunfighter at the OK Corral'*.

The other member of our four-ball was Jack 'Jacko' Maloney. He was a rheumatologist, who had treated my mother and had been a friend of my father in earlier days. Jack had played rugby for Ireland on a number of occasions as a front row forward, despite his weight and size being much less than would be required today. On one occasion after Australia had played (and beaten) Ireland he was talking in the bar at Portmarnock golf club with John Eales, the giant Australian second row forward and captain. Somebody mentioned to Eales that Jack had played for Ireland in his day. *'Is that so, what position did you play'*?, asked the Australian. Conscious of the fact that his weight was 13st. compared to Eales' 18st. Jacko replied, *'Scrum-half'*.

Our games of golf were intensely competitive but once they were over friendship was resumed. On one occasion at the European Club, Noel Walsh and I fought in a particularly feisty four-ball against Jack Maloney and George Duffy. We were all square on the 18th when George hit his ball into the edge of a hazard just in front of the 18th green. We called a penalty on him, which he disputed, saying his ball was visible and in fact just outside the hazard. We played out the hole, feeling we had won the match by a stroke, assuming that our calling of the penalty was correct. Jack and George would not agree and Gerry Ruddy, the son of the European Club's owner, was called on to adjudicate. The ball was duly replaced. Gerry determined that it was indeed in the hazard and that a penalty shot should be incurred. Our opponents still would not agree and requested Gerry to place the matter before the Golfing Union of Ireland (GUI) for a decision, documented by photographs. We then all repaired to the clubhouse dining room for a most jovial and sociable meal. I have no idea what the outcome of the referral to the GUI was, if indeed it was ever referred. Our golf games were sometimes like this and I do not know what I would have done without them.

Chapter 11

Back to Belvedere

Belvedere College and its ethos of Jesuit education with its constant refrain of encouragement to be *'Men for Others'* was probably the greatest influence on my life. The power of this idea and the full recognition of the responsibility that goes with privilege were slow to come to fruition for me but when it did it became the litmus test for my choices in life.

The Jesuits are firstly men of God. My good friend Fr. Joe Dargan SJ. used to say that there was a small part of him reserved only for God and that nobody else could access that. I was asked on occasion if I would make the Spiritual Exercises of Saint Ignatius and I declined because I did not feel comfortable with this. For me, such deep faith is a gift and, although I do believe in God, I had not been favoured with the gift of faith as it is understood in the Catholic Church. I should say that I think atheism does not make any sense; it is quite simply impossible to be sure that there is no God. Once when Keyna and I were holidaying in Dornoch, on the wild and beautiful north-east of Scotland, we went to a service in the Church of Scotland (Presbyterian) tradition. It so happened that the homily of the day was given in front of the church elders and all of the congregation by a man who was an applicant for the vacant position of Pastor. In his homily he acknowledged that he was still searching and that he did not know for certain that God existed; but he was searching in good faith and would continue to do so. I liked this humility. My God is unknowable to me but I also continue to search. I can recall an occasion at the annual convocation of the boards of Irish Jesuit schools when, during a discussion on social justice, some held the view that good works without faith are of a lesser value. I disagree; in fact, I think there is a case to be made for good works without faith being of a higher order. Fr. Joe was a very saintly man and yet he was robust in secular matters. He was completely non-judgmental and he had great faith in, and hopes for, me. If I am ever gifted with true faith it will be due to him.

When I was at school in the late 1950s almost all of the teaching staff were Jesuit priests. By the 1990s vocations to the priesthood were rare and the school now increasingly relied on lay teachers. Despite this the ethos of education remained constant. What appealed to me most was Belvedere's extraordinary commitment to social justice, always achieved in a calm, reflective, and fulfilling way that was in sharp contrast to the shrill voices of some (although also well motivated). The Jesuits have been described as 'Contemplatives in Action' and I think this accurately describes the role of these fine men at the school.

Fr. Joe Dargan SJ.

The so-called *'Belvedere Family'* also included the teachers, students, parents and the past pupils, primarily through the Past Pupils Union, and many others who were attracted to the vision. Belvedere was a good school when I attended it; it is now a great school. Its growth and evolution has been hugely influenced by its location. In a very real sense Belvedere has been *'meeting its neighbours in the street'* and this has substantially influenced the social justice traditions of the school and its Past.

I had no contact with Belvedere, and very little contact with former classmates, for a long time after leaving in 1956 and heading off to Bailieborough to begin my banking career. But the legacy of the values that had been drilled into me has been a huge influence on my life. Other aspects were the importance of developing God-given gifts and talents, and also the idea of lifelong learning.

Life throws up things at the oddest times and in the most surprising ways. I had many friends among IIB's customers in the corporate sector; a particularly close one was Jim King, one of the senior executives in GPA. Jim and his lovely wife, Maeve, invited Keyna and I to their home in Limerick for some merriment and to attend a charity fundraising dinner at Adare Manor Hotel. Their other house guests were Karl and Doreen Mullen, a wonderful couple who soon became good friends of ours. In the early 1950's Karl had captained the British and Irish Lions rugby touring team. The fundraising dinner was a great success and a memorable evening was had by the six of us. I developed an immediate rapport with Karl Mullen and over breakfast the following morning he said to me, *'Paddy, how come you have never become involved with the Belvedere Old Boys? We are going to have to do something about that. I'm the incoming President of our College Union and want you to help me. So how about taking on the captaincy of the Union's Golfing Society'?*

I told him that I had never been asked before and would be very happy to become involved. What neither of us appreciated was that that is not the way in which one becomes captain of the Union Golf Society! Shortly afterwards I was invited into Belvedere College for lunch to meet the Rector, Michael Shiel SJ., and Karl. We met in the parlour and when a glass of wine was put in my hand I had the

241

sense that a door had been quietly locked. Over the most convivial conversation I was asked if I would chair a committee of past pupils and others to raise money to build new premises for the Belvedere Youth Club (BYC). I had the impression I was not to be let out until I agreed. I was assured the amount in question was of the order of £180,000. The actual figure turned out to be £650,000 (this was before the introduction of the euro).

The Belvedere Youth Club, the oldest and largest youth club in Dublin, has long dedicated itself to improving the lives of young people living in one of Dublin's disadvantaged areas. When I became involved it had more than 400 young members and the plan was to build dedicated new premises to include facilities for arts

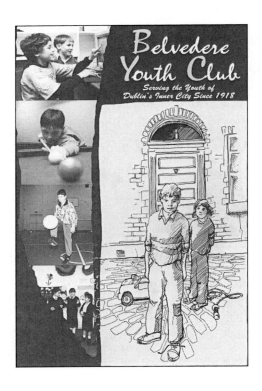

and crafts, computer skills, snooker, gym activities, table tennis, debating, drama etc. In 1918, under the guidance of the Belvedere Union, which was originally called the Belvedere Social Services Club, its life began in Harry Street. In the early years famous past Belvederians such as Eugene Davy, one of the founders of Davy Stockbrokers and William Lombard Murphy, Chairman of Irish Independent Newspapers provided the leadership. In 1926 its name was changed to the Belvedere Newsboys' Club. One of its early missions was to provide shoes for desperately poor and barefooted young boys who were selling newspapers around the streets of Dublin. When Eugene Davy wrote to congratulate me on the success of the fundraising, he recalled that, '*In 1921, together with a few others I helped in locating the original club in Grattan Court off Mount Street. It was a coachman's premises donated by a Mr. Meleady who owned carriage horses. The boys were newsboys, many of them in their bare feet. They earned 3d for the sale of a dozen papers, each costing one penny. They mainly came from tenement houses, one family to a room*'.

Corporate philanthropy was not well established in Ireland in the early 1990s and raising the sort of money required for new premises was a daunting challenge but we had one great advantage, the Belvedere family. I have to say that, despite all my experience of raising money for Irish Intercontinental Bank Ltd in the early 1970s, I hated fundraising. I started by setting up subcommittees targeting different segments of the market, each with its own chairman and financial goal. These included the corporate sector, the financial services sector, the Belvedere parents and the Belvedere Past. There was also a variety of events including a golf classic, concerts, and other 'happenings'.

Our initial objective was to kick-start the project by finding some major donors and I took responsibility for this sub-committee. We had in mind that these so-called special gifts would be of the order of £25,000 each. I was very grateful to my own bank for agreeing to be the first donor; AIB and Bank of Ireland followed suit, as did a number of high-net-worth individuals, including clients of AIB who had been approached by Brian Wilson, then a senior executive with the bank. As I have already recounted, Bertie Ahern was instrumental in getting Guinness involved. The Club was of course in his constituency but I was always impressed by his genuine commitment to social justice causes whenever I met him.

I also met with Ben Dunne, then the CEO of Dunne's Stores, in my office one day and at the end of the business discussion I told him about the fundraising drive for the youth club and asked could he consider supporting it financially. *'How much do you want'*? He asked. I gulped and said we were hoping that some institutions or individuals might give as much as £25,000. He took out his cheque book and wrote a personal cheque in that amount on the spot.

I was really inspired by the way in which Belvedere responded to the call; both the school and the union put no limits on the support they gave. The golf classic was organised by Niall O'Carroll, and a concert by Karl and Doreen Mullen. We reached our target in about a year, with the special-gifts initiative contributing in excess of

£250,000, the corporate sector and individual donations an additional £200,000, and various events and other sources in excess of £200,000. The campaign had been kick-started by a memorable midsummer garden party hosted by Karl and Doreen, while Keyna and I hosted an evening at our home for campaign volunteers.

On 25 September 1992, the new premises were formally opened and blessed by the Provincial of the Jesuit order in Ireland, Laurence Murphy SJ. Bertie Ahern, by this time Minister for Finance, unveiled a commemorative plaque and remarked that the fundraising effort was one of the most effective he had seen in his time in public office. He also told us that he had prevailed upon the Minister for the Environment to donate £15,000 from a fund at his disposal.

Tony O'Reilly presenting a cheque to the Belvedere Youth Club.
Also attending, Tim Sheehy and Fr. Michael Shiel SJ.

The official opening of the Belvedere Youth Club's new premises attended by Minister for Finance, Bertie Ahern TD and Fr. Lawrence Murphy SJ. Provincial of the Irish Jesuits.

About 250 people attended this formal opening, and that same evening about 200 former and current club members came in, as much for a social evening as to see around the building. Tony O'Reilly, who had given a generous personal gift, also spoke and I remember him saying, *'A friend in need is a pain in the ass'*. That was my job!

It was Karl Mullen who had been responsible for my coming back to the Belvedere family and this was to be a labour of love for me. The Jesuits have a particular skill in holding on to people, in getting you to do more and more; they have absolutely no shame in asking because they see their mission as doing God's work. In my case asking was easy. Looking back I can unhesitatingly say that I owed Belvedere College much more than the school could ever have got from me.

I became involved in all sorts of Belvedere-related projects over the next fifteen years including chairing committees, helping to put financial structures in place and yes, fundraising, again! I suppose I did feel at times that I was bringing some leadership to the table but the real leadership was always the school, the Jesuits and their vision. All I did was embrace this vision as a willing follower.

Belvedere styles its social justice initiatives under the heading of what it terms a Social Diversity Programme; it was and is multifaceted and embraces:

- The Belvedere Youth Club
- The Belvedere Benevolent Association, run by the Past Pupils Union, which provides confidential assistance to members of the Past and their dependents who are in need
- Fr. Peter McVerry's hostels for homeless boys
- A scholarship scheme for boys from disadvantaged areas designed to provide free education throughout the full senior cycle for up to 10 per cent of the school's overall intake.

Students are encouraged to become involved in practical ways such as working with the Society of St Vincent de Paul, fundraising, and as transition year students helping as volunteers at the youth club.

Belvedere was fortunate to have an outstanding and creative Headmaster at the time, Fr. Leonard Moloney SJ. I joined the school's board of management and chaired its finance committee in 1993. I found that the finances were in a bad way and the control systems were not fit for purpose. Fr. Leonard was later to refer to them as '*shambolic*'. With the help of Nick Sparrow, the recruitment of Mary Brady as Bursar, and with the active support and encouragement of the board and Headmaster we helped in putting the finances on a sound footing for future years. In classic Belvedere tradition, once the problems and the solutions were identified, the board and the school Trustee were fully supportive.

The physical plant at the school was also felt to be in need of renewal, and the board was exercised about developing a master plan for future generations. Belvedere College was now about to enter a period of exceptional dynamism. The ambitious plan was to be in two distinct phases: the first involved the construction of a multipurpose theatre/assembly hall together with the construction of an underground car park and a landscaped courtyard, the second concentrated on building a new science and technology block. We needed money, a great deal of it, and the first task was to put in place a fundraising drive to finance the estimated £5 million or more required for the first phase of the work. I was asked to act as co-chair of this fundraising drive together with the Rector, Joe Dargan SJ, and the Headmaster. Fundraising again, but despite the challenge I did feel privileged be involved.

The Jesuits were full of optimism for the task but I worried that too much reliance might be placed on the past pupils who, with notable exceptions, were not a particularly wealthy group. We needed and got help in the form of professional fundraisers. These people were good, they were very experienced. They knew how to put a proper structure in place and were ruthless in the difficult task of asking for money. They were also very expensive. A range of subcommittees was again put in place reporting to the joint chairs, and we in turn reported to the board, which was responsible to the Provincial of the Jesuit order in Ireland, as Trustee.

The Jesuit Order gave a large donation to start the fundraising drive, and the new committees were focused on major gifts, the Belvedere Past, past and present parents, and a relentless series of events, sporting and musical. At an early stage, Fr. Joe went to see that illustrious Old Belvederian, A.J.F. O'Reilly, at his Castlemartin residence to ask for his help. Tony, an exceptional man and renowned philanthropist, responded positively and generously.

Fr. Joe and I made countless visits to targeted donors, mostly from the ranks of the Past. He used to tell me before we started that he had prayed for success at his morning Mass. Regularly, we would be asked what the expected level of donation was. Without batting an eyelid, Joe would reply that so-and-so had given £100,000. Joe was equally impressed with very small contributions, and I remember him being very excited about one for a few euros from someone who was impoverished.

One visit was to Paddy Campbell, the then owner of Bewley's café. After we had made our pitch, Paddy said to us *'Do you gentlemen realise that I was expelled from Belvedere in my day'*? I was highly embarrassed at this stage, but Joe simply asked, *'What were the reasons, Paddy'*? Apparently, Paddy Campbell had been expelled for two reasons; firstly, he had submitted anonymous letters to the *Evening Mail* lampooning some of the teaching staff, and, secondly, he had formed an Elvis Presley fan club at school. I think you might get a medal for such activities today. He gave us a generous contribution towards the appeal.

The fundraising drive was relentless, and in particular the unfortunate parent group was regularly harangued by the Headmaster and by my good friend, Tim Sheehy. I felt sorry for them. If you had any connections to Belvedere in those days, you would have been wise to go on an extended holiday or even emigrate but, of course, the parents were a particularly vulnerable group given that their sons were in the school. Little by little we reached our target but because some committed contributions were slow to be honoured there was a residual bank debt for some time.

The O'Reilly Theatre was and is one of the finest in the city and over the years has hosted many prestigious events. The car park has been a profitable activity for Belvedere for many years. The fundraising project was exhausting and exhilarating and I made enduring friendships with past Belvederians and others who, like me, were inspired by the mission of the school and the Jesuits.

These were men of wit, generosity and talent like Tim Sheehy, P. J. McAllister, Tom Byrne and Eugene Dunne.

I particularly enjoyed meeting up again with classmates from my year, 1956. My great friend John McGilligan, now deceased and whom I greatly miss, had, together with Tom Prior, taken responsibility for fundraising from a particular group of past pupils on the condition, *'We do it our way and no interference'*. This was fine with me; they did it their way and very successfully. And then there were Denis McDowell and Paddy Shortall who had moved to Clongowes and Castleknock, respectively, midway through the senior cycle. I have great memories of their partying at our holiday home in Wexford. McDowell and Shortall were always winding each other up. On one occasion Shortall, after a few glasses of vino, was describing this exclusive dining club which he had been invited to join. He explained that the criteria for membership were very stringent, including being either a good judge of food and wine, being an outstanding conversationalist, or being a gentleman. McDowell quickly enquired as to which of these three criteria ensured Shortall's membership!

In 2002, the centenary year of the school union, I had the great honour to be its President. The annals of the union and the school are a treasure trove of memories. In my first contribution to the union newsletter, I recalled that the 1941 edition of *The Belvederian*, in celebrating the centenary of the purchase of Belvedere House, contained an essay which opens thus:

'The stately townhouse of my Lord Belvedere had been closed for some little time until one day in 1841 mild excitement was caused in the vicinity by preparation for its reopening. The neighbourhood had missed the stream of carriages and chairs, the coming and going of the beauty and the fashion of the polite Society of Dublin city, and was glad to look forward to the pageantry which could be had so cheaply. It was doomed to disappointment, for when the doors of Belvedere House were thrown open once again the neighbourhood was treated to the unusual sight of Catholic boys going to school openly, unusual, because Mr. O'Connell's Emancipation act was not so very old, and the former evil days not far gone when Catholics must creep to their disguised academies furtively and fearfully less Dublin Castle lay its heavy hand on their schools and on their masters'.

I chaired the centenary executive meeting of the union on 19 June 2002. Past Presidents and those associated with the school's sporting and social activities were invited guests, and each, in turn, spoke to special memories. Because of Karl Mullen's advancing years I had difficulty in persuading him to attend, and it was only when I offered to send a car for him that he relented. He made me promise that I would not call on him to speak. When it was the rugby club's turn to address the meeting there was silence, everybody presuming that Karl would wish to speak. Eventually, the President of the rugby club stood up to speak about the great exploits of the Old Belvedere rugby club over the past decades.

Attendees at the centenary executive meeting of the Belvedere Past Pupils Union on 19th June 2002 include the following:

Tim Sheehy, Fr. Joe Dargan SJ., Diarmuid O'Heagerty, Charlie O'Connell, Pat Feenan, Fr. Leonard Moloney SJ., Paddy McEvoy, Padraig Ingoldsby, Brian Merry, Gerard Long, Sean Gannon, Reggie Jackson, Roddy Fitzpatrick, Martin Ryan, Paul Hussey, Ken Doyle, Ron Skelly, Luke McKeever, Berchmans Gannon, Brendan O'Leary, Damian O'Neill, Vinny Duffy, Dermot Lavelle, John O'Connor, Karl Mullen, David Ross, Donal Birthistle, Gerry Walsh, Brendan Heneghan, Oisin Coghlan, Don Larkin, Padraig Murray, Fr. Bruce Bradley SJ., Fintan Synnott, John Kirwan and Diarmuid Moore.

He was just getting into his stride when Karl stood up and said, '*I think I'd like to say a few words here*'.

After that I could not get him to stop; he went on and on, anecdote after anecdote. One I remember is about the famous Quinn brothers; apparently one of them (I think it was Gerry) was chosen to play for Ireland and on the Friday night before the Saturday game he rang the IRFU to make apologies for the fact that he would have to cry off because he would not be in Dublin on the day. However, he kindly suggested that his brother Paddy would be very happy to play in his place.

In later years, Fr. Leonard was to congratulate me on what he called '*personal courage*' in the decision to change the annual dinner venue from the Burlington to Jury's Hotel despite '*formidable logistical and other obsta*cles'. I had no choice; the original venue became impossible when Cardinal Desmond Connell was unable to attend on the planned date. The alternative was Jury's Hotel and initially they informed us that our proposed new date did not suit them, but good fortune was with me and at the last moment the hotel had a cancellation and we got the slot. The dinner is usually the highlight of the presidency; 400 members of the Past attended, eminent guests included the Cardinal, board members and teachers and the Presidents of fellow secondary schools in the Dublin area as well as special guests, including the great Jack Kyle and Olympic gold medallist, Ronnie Delany.

A favourite photograph, with former classmates on the occasion of the Past Pupils Union Annual Dinner.

I was terrified at the prospect of making a speech to this distinguished gathering. I remember going to the bathroom just before I was due to speak, simply to compose myself, and meeting John Kirwan, who greatly relaxed me, saying, '*Paddy, don't forget everyone in the room is on your side and wants you to do well and to enjoy yourself*'. In the event I did enjoy myself and probably made one of the best speeches of my life.

In 2003, I was invited by the Provincial to chair the College Board for the next three years. I had exceptional board colleagues and Belvedere had another outstanding new Headmaster. After ten years of contribution to Belvedere and its ethos, Fr. Leonard moved to Clongowes Wood College, and the school was incredibly fortunate in recruiting the first non-Jesuit head, Gerry Foley, to take over from him. Like his predecessor, Gerry is a charismatic man and,

Gerry Foley

although not a Jesuit, he fully embraced all that the Jesuits stood for. It became a seamless transition and it was such a pleasure to work with him throughout my years as Chairman. We were a great team and became firm friends. The first phase of the development plan was now complete and fully funded, and a second phase of fundraising had been established, under Brian Kearney's chairmanship, to facilitate the planned new science and technology park and a university-style science lecture theatre. The board was heavily involved in all aspects of this second phase of the plans.

In my final year in the chair, the Jesuit community moved to Gardiner Street, and from then on there was no longer a Jesuit community presence at Belvedere's Great Denmark Street address. The college's 174-year-old Jesuit legacy was commemorated at a function in May 2006 when we presented a special manuscript to the Jesuit Provincial, John Dardis SJ. The manuscript was in the format of a book containing a vellum page for every year of Jesuit service at Belvedere. It included the names of all the priests, brothers, and scholastics in the college from 1832 to 2006, and it noted their professional duties. The manuscript itself is a work of art, beautifully handwritten in italic script by two calligraphers.

This was a sad occasion for us and we wanted to thank the Jesuits for the gift of Belvedere and for the legacy of a community presence at the school. They would continue to be close by at Gardiner Street but it would not be quite the same. It will be a challenge to keep Belvedere Jesuit in future years.

I spoke then of the gratitude of the Past and the friendships among alumni, whose formation and mission was to follow the social justice traditions of the Jesuits. I talked about a wonderful book, *Heroic Leadership,* written by Chris Lowney, a former Jesuit novice who worked in the top echelons of the banking group J. P. Morgan for 17 years. He wrote about the leadership principles that guided the Jesuits for more than 450 years: self-awareness, ingenuity, openess to change, love and heroism. He described the

Jesuit mission as being about transforming our society based on love, faith, solidarity with the poor, the search for excellence, and fidelity. He reminded us that St Ignatius placed great emphasis on the importance of schools in the early mission of the Jesuits and that the early Jesuits recognised that students would have a better prospect of discovering God in all things through a synthesis of faith and culture within schools. This remains the task today.

I recalled that the encouragement for the formation of the union originally came from Fr. Nicholas Tompkins SJ., then Headmaster. The inaugural meeting took place on 14 March 1902 when among those attending was Christopher Pallas, the Lord Chief Baron, and Stanislaus Joyce, head boy and brother of James Joyce, who sent an apology. During the meeting, Sir Francis Cruise, the distinguished physician, noted that the school's mission was to restore self-respect for things Irish. *The Belvederian* of the day noted also that he congratulated the Rector on recently abolishing corporal punishment at the school; regrettably a decision not persevered with according to my own experience at the school. I also recalled that Sir Francis contributed an article to the inaugural issue of *The Belvederian* (1906) in which he tells a little story about the Headmaster, Fr. Meagher, which deserves retelling:

'Good Fr. Meagher loved the boys and won their affection and esteem despite his exterior reserve, and he was always ready to take the part of anyone in trouble. I will relate to you a story to illustrate his character. One day a very fine lady called to consult him, confidentially, about a great trouble

which weighed heavily on her soul. Awful to relate she had discovered that her son was actually in the same class with her baker's son. "Let me hope dear Fr. Meagher", she said, "that you will take precautions that no undue intimacy shall arise between these two boys". Make your mind easy, dear madam" quote his reverence; "it is true that the boys are in the same class, but, as the baker's son is always at the top and your son equally punctually at the bottom, you need not apprehend any close intimacy arising between them". The lady retired, silenced if not comforted'.

I got to know a great Jesuit, Fr. Derek Cassidy SJ., who had replaced Fr. Joe as Rector. As Rector, Derek had a vitally important role to play in the life of Belvedere and at our board meetings. Notwithstanding all the issues we had to face, including sometimes fraught issues in the daily life of the school, I think we were unanimous on every occasion when we had to make an important decision.

A huge preoccupation for us was the Scholarship Scheme, for this more than anything else defined what Belvedere was about. The best antidote to poverty and disadvantage is education, and this unique scheme, started in 1986, provided six years free education at Belvedere for 90 boys. The word 'Scholarship' is somewhat of a misnomer, since the only requirement is that boys offered scholarships would be able to benefit from the school's educational offerings. Much more significant criteria were the inability to pay and a supportive attitude from parents and family. The scheme is fully embedded into the life of Belvedere and it enriches both the scholar and the school as a whole. The support of the teachers, the student body, and the parents is manifest, and the success of the scheme is tangible: 90 per cent of scholars complete secondary education, 72 per cent go on to third level education, and 22 per cent to postgraduate studies.

At the time, the percentage of scholarship students at Belvedere was just over 9 per cent, against a target of 10 per cent. The funding requirements were huge, being of the order of £400,000 per annum. Initially, the Jesuit community had generously gifted the programme, and over the years a capital fund had been built up with the dividend going towards the scheme's costs. The balance had to be raised by further fundraising if the capital fund itself was not to be depleted. But these were the Celtic Tiger years and the capital fund began to perform handsomely. The Jesuit Province was now keen to increase the admissions target to 15 per cent of the annual school intake. I was against this for two reasons: firstly, I felt that an intake at this level might unbalance what Belvedere was offering to the fee-paying parents and, even more importantly, I was concerned about the financial implications. We debated it on a number of occasions, and it was decided to defer further consideration of increasing the number of students until the capital fund was on a much stronger footing. Only a few years later the economic recession decimated the capital fund, and this created significant new challenges for future boards.

I never went into a board meeting without advance discussion and agreement, firstly with the Headmaster and Rector, and then with any other party who was likely to hold strong views on an agenda item. I'm told I did a good job as chair, and I'm also told that I was known for taking off my wristwatch, and placing it on the table and crossing my legs, which was apparently understood to be a signal that the talking was to stop and the meeting to come to an end. I'm not sure how true this is.

In 2006 two things happened which gave me particular satisfaction. The first was that Belvedere won both the senior and junior Leinster rugby cups, and the second was that in my last year as chair both the school captain and its vice-captain were scholarship boys.

Joy for all past Belvederians when the school won both the Senior and Junior Cups. The two captains, Conor Colclough and Robert Carson with the cups.

At the end of my term I was asked by the Provincial to consider extending it for a further three-year period. I declined, feeling at this stage that I had given my all to Belvedere and after 15 years I was tired.

Keyna and I celebrated 50 years of marriage in 2014, and we arranged for a Mass to be said by our three Jesuit friends, Joe, Leonard, and Derek at our home, to be attended by close friends and extended family. Fr. Joe was to be the main celebrant, but shortly before the Mass he contacted me with the very distressing news that he had been diagnosed with cancer and was now in palliative care at the Blackrock Clinic. In his absence Fr. Derek gave a beautiful homily, in which he said that Joe had instructed him to say that I had brought great integrity and Christian values to my professional and business career. It really meant a lot to me to hear my friends pay tribute to the values I tried to bring to my work. Joe died a short time later; when I visited him in hospital, his concern was always only for Keyna and me and for those he was leaving. He was totally resigned, and he told me, *'If this is what God wants from me now, then that's fine with me'*.

As I was completing this memoir we had a visit to our home from Leonard Moloney SJ., now ten years Headmaster at Clongowes Wood College. We had talked about books and many other things, when Leonard said to me, *'Paddy, the Jesuit community has a significant farm attached to Clongowes. It is 350 acres of prime land with a herd of 300 cows on it. We were wondering would you be willing to take over the chairmanship of this enterprise'?* This was extraordinary; I had always wanted to be a farmer . . .

Chapter 12

A Digression
Reflections on the Banking Crisis

Banks have unique opportunities to contribute to society's needs. They also have unique responsibilities to do so because they are highly privileged institutions. Entrance to the industry is highly restricted. When Irish Intercontinental Bank (IIB's precursor) was formed in 1973 the only reason we were given a banking licence by the Central Bank was because of the failure of a small Irish bank (Irish International Bank) and our commitment to the Receiver to purchase certain assets and contribute to potential losses. Banks are granted a special status in gathering retail deposits. They are also given privileged access to the Central Bank as lender of last resort, and as we have seen recently if they fail there is the prospect of recapitalisation from the government. The permitted ratio of their loan assets to their shareholder funds is a multiple of that which would apply to an unregulated and unlicensed institution.

Obligations follow these privileges, independently of any moral responsibility to operate the business in a principled manner. The main obligation of a bank is to ensure that it is adequately capitalised and that business is conducted in a manner which protects its depositors. But banks also have a responsibility to ensure that their business model has an appropriate focus on lending to the real economy, and that appropriate risk management procedures are in place. These are in theory shareholder responsibilities, but in our modern economy the shareholders are far removed from the day-to-day running of the banks so these tasks are delegated to the boards of directors and to the senior executives.

Banks have never been popular. However, a new level of unpopularity was reached for Irish banks when they became an object of contempt and hatred following the recent economic crisis. We witnessed an unremitting attempt to build short-term banking profitability, through apparently high return lending focused on the property sector. And this new approach led to the frequent abandonment of well-proven risk management procedures.

It is hard to believe that as recently as 2006 the international consulting company Mercer Oliver Wyman (MOW), in launching its annual assessment of the world financial services industry at the World Economic Forum in Davos, ranked Anglo Irish Bank (Anglo) at the head of its global rankings for the period 2001–5. Moreover this was not the first time that Anglo had shone in global rankings. Anglo was the poster boy at the time and its success story and financial model were lauded internationally and domestically. On the home front it was regularly praised by the financial press, by government ministers and other well-known public representatives. This cheerleading motivated many in the Irish banking industry to follow the Anglo model which at that time was one of concentrating lending on major developers with whom they had built a strong business relationship. No doubt there was also pressure from institutional shareholders, viewing the Anglo returns enviously.

All three investigations established by the Irish government to look into the causes of the crisis (Regling Watson, Honohan, and Nyberg) concluded that while international developments and regulatory shortfalls facilitated the crisis to some degree, the root cause lay at home. The Irish banking industry was largely responsible for its own downfall. The failure of so-called *'Light touch'* regulation was also recognised as a key contributory factor. In this, we followed the American model, popularised by Alan Greenspan during his term as Chairman of the US Federal Reserve Bank. The approach relied on the market to provide self-correcting mechanisms. The market failed to do so in the United States, or in Ireland, or anywhere else for that matter. Irish regulatory oversight failed in a particular way. Not only was there a failure to effectively regulate individual banks, especially Anglo and Irish Nationwide (INBS) but even more importantly the authorities did not read or respond to the macroeconomic signals. The over-rapid growth in lending should have been a clear marker. With hindsight it is clear that consideration was not given to the impact on the Irish banks of the explosion of domestic credit at the lower interest rates resulting from membership of the euro.

Blaming the Regulator is not an excuse; it is for each individual bank to set and follow its own prudential standards. Boards of banking institutions as well as their senior executives had clear responsibilities here. The board, in particular, was and is supposed to monitor the behaviour of the senior executives. The investigative reports make clear that the traditional culture and values within the banking industry were regularly abandoned. In earlier times banks were criticised for being too focused on risk management and insufficiently motivated to help entrepreneurship and risk-taking. There was some validity in this criticism. Certainly, there is a need for banks to support risk-taking and new ventures, but getting this balance right is always a considerable challenge. However, it can never be an excuse for the wide-scale relaxation of risk management rules.

In the early 1970s the collapse of the secondary banking system in the UK triggered a crisis for Irish property companies and started a recessionary environment which lasted for many years, coincidentally the time when IIB Bank was started. There were big lessons to be learned then about the need to focus on good quality lending. Why do we keep forgetting?

Banks do not have the right, mandate, or authority to use their resources aggressively to create short-term shareholder value. On the contrary the focus must always be on sustainable long-term returns, the logic of the marathon rather than the sprint. An altogether different dimension to this issue arises when senior bank management is given a vested interest in short-term profitability because of ill-designed compensation systems, pay, bonuses, stock options and pension plans.

I have two principal criticisms of the Irish banking industry. The first is the compensation structures which encouraged a culture of greed and short-term approaches. The second is that of mismanagement in what were traditional areas of strength such as risk management and funding models.

When compensation schemes are designed to encourage a sales culture, with large payouts earned over the short term and with no recognition of the potential for loss in later years, they are a recipe for the type of lending which prevailed within the Irish banking industry. A short-term sales-driven culture easily leads to rule bending to achieve targets. I am in favour of compensation systems designed to attract high quality employees, and of encouraging share ownership within the employee group. I also believe there is merit in bonus schemes so long as they are aligned with medium-term strategic plans and are set at reasonable levels, with payouts restricted until the medium-term.

The over-reliance on short-term money market sources rather than the traditional stable deposits to finance the acquisition of high-risk and long-term assets was shown to be a deeply flawed funding model. For many years this type of funding was too easily available to Irish banks, both from within and outside the Eurozone. When these facilities were finally withdrawn following the collapse of Lehman Brothers in September 2008 liquidity dried up and the Irish banks had to turn to the Irish and European Central Banks for funding support. This liquidity crisis rapidly progressed to a solvency crisis as the poor quality of some of the loans was exposed. Debt write-downs left the banks dramatically short of adequate capital.

Irish banks were not alone in causing economic devastation. In the American market, in particular, there are examples in both the investment and commercial banks of activities which many allege to be criminal, for example, investment banks as well-known as Goldman Sachs and Merrill Lynch packaged and sold complex bonds known as collateralised debt obligations (CDOs). The portfolios in these bonds comprised some very dubious mortgage loans, including the so-called 'liar loans' made to borrowers who had no income, no jobs and no assets; people in receipt of a mortgage were invited to fill out their own financial details, no checks were in place and no documentation was required. The Wall Street banks persuaded the rating agencies to apply a triple-A rating to these CDOs, arguing that the risks involved were distributed throughout the whole of the United States and that, surely, they could not all fail at the same time. They did.

Essentially, CDOs had become a dumping ground for bonds that could not be sold on their own. As former Goldman Sachs commercial mortgage backed securities surveillance expert Mike Blum explained: *'Wall Street made huge profits from creating filet mignon AAAs out of BB manure'*. Worse was to come as some Wall Street institutions, believing their CDOs would fail, bet against them in the market, booking the resulting profit. The fraudulent behaviour of Wall Street financial institutions has now been well documented. These institutions made enormous profits and their executives received huge bonuses, and essentially no one has been held to account for these deeply dishonest practices.

Under pressure from the government, Irish banks began, very reluctantly, to lend money for home loans in the 1970s. Prior to that this was the preserve of the Building Societies which were mutual societies funded by personal deposits. Lending for the acquisition of residential properties has gathered momentum in recent decades and is now regarded as a worthy activity. By the late 1990s, cultural and economic factors were at play in the apparently insatiable demand and the attendant rise in prices that prevailed for residential mortgage borrowing. Social shifts in family formation contributed to the additional demand and the declining average age of first-time buyers created a surge in new potential buyers. There were, however, unacceptable excesses in what became a frenzy of lending for house acquisition, including lending of 100 per cent and more of loan to value, interest-only mortgages and aggressive equity release products.

When the bubble burst, house prices fell by on average 50 per cent and unemployment levels rose from 4 per cent to nearly 15 per cent. The changed economic circumstances meant that many who had taken out mortgages to buy homes could not now afford the repayments, causing great hardship and pain. Banks have a significant level of responsibility here and do have an obligation to take this into account when looking for solutions in the case of distressed borrowers.

And what of the future for Irish banks, which, like many of their European counterparts, have been brought back to health only by the infusion of massive amounts of equity capital funded from the public purse? Having lived through other banking crises in the past the thing that stands out most for me is that people forget. When the good times come people expect them to continue indefinitely and they do not. Poor risk management, excessive leverage, inadequate regulation and doubtful business practices may well return. Unfortunately, the industry does not have a self-regulating agency such as exists within the medical and legal fraternities. The Banking and Payments Federation Ireland (BPFI), formerly IBF, can be effective as a lobby group or for public relations purposes but has no mandate to regulate the industry from within. If real change is to come about, then it must come from the philosophy and leadership provided by individual banks, and this must primarily come from the larger institutions.

The banking industry should recognise the privileged position of banks and the obligations this entails. The first challenge is to embrace a principled leadership model, one which recognises responsibilities to all stakeholders including staff, customers, shareholders and the community at large. The challenge is to build a business model which is based on long-term sustainable success in parallel with growth and prosperity in the economy.

In particular, there needs to be a recognition that the small and medium-sized business sector (SME) is the main provider of jobs in the Irish economy and without adequate funding for this sector sustainable economic growth will be compromised. I believe there is a genuine opportunity for the banking industry in Ireland to take a sustained role in the provision of reasonably priced finance to the

SME sector. There is also much more that can be done to encourage in practical ways innovation and entrepreneurship. It is clearly in the interests of the banking industry to focus on a business model which seeks to build the financial strength of the nation. It can even make a contribution to a gradual re-establishment of trust between banks and the people.

The Irish economy is a mixed market economy, not a pure market economy unfettered by government intervention. However, the capitalist ethic has been strongly to the fore and in the *Index of Economic Freedom* 2015, Ireland is ranked number nine in the world (and third of the 43 European countries surveyed). Over time capitalism has shown itself to be an unmatched system for building wealth, improving efficiency, encouraging innovation and fostering growth. The capitalist system is now under siege; 'the market' is less and less thought of as a universal panacea. Business is increasingly viewed as being responsible for social, environmental and economic problems and many are of the view that business prospers at the expense of society at large.

The recent economic crisis was facilitated by market participants collaborating tacitly. The banking industry, the property sector, real estate valuation firms and auditors, all played their part alongside government and regulatory agencies. One of the problems of a market system is that it tends to concentrate power in the hands of a small number of participants who can then manipulate the rules of the game. When the banks and some of their principal customers in the property sector felt they saw the opportunity for exceptional advantage the system enabled this without consideration for the longer term consequences for the community at large. Real estate valuation firms took fees for valuations which became rapidly unsustainable, and the accountancy profession took fees for effectively giving a clean bill of health to banks, in some instances as little as six months before they had to be bailed out. And government was happy to rely on the construction sector taxes as a major source of revenue; it was the collapse of property-related tax revenues that was the occasion of the fiscal crisis. The government actively supported the market over an extended period. Its agencies benignly allowed unhealthy concentrations of lending in high-risk areas, unsustainable short-term funding for long-term assets, and regular relaxations of the credit standards that had served the banking industry well in earlier times.

The failure of the capitalist market system to serve society's needs has the inevitable and understandable consequence of increasing the appeal of alternative socio-political models such as liberalism and socialism. These do have a contribution to make to our mixed market economy and often the agendas of those described as 'left wing' can capture the imagination of the public and encourage government to introduce liberal and socially advantageous policies. In Europe and the US we have seen moves towards gender equality and social change, and areas such as the rising minimum wage are gaining the attention of politicians on both sides of the political divide. Here in Ireland welfare reform, education and gender equality have all been influenced positively by the liberal perspective. I have experienced the consequences of state socialism in both the Czech Republic and Hungary and have seen how it creates power elites, and how it stifles innovation, enterprise and growth. On the other hand, the Western world cannot afford for our economic model based on capitalism to fail so dramatically again. If our economic system continues to be unfit for purpose and promote vast and growing wealth inequality we may anticipate that it will be replaced by alternative models. The process is already underway and it should be a clarion call to action.

Capitalist-based economic models have been with us since the 16th century and their evolution has been influenced by liberal and social philosophies. New ideas are again afoot, initially led by academics such as Michael Porter of the Harvard Business School. Now, campuses on major American business schools and more importantly enlightened companies, General Electric and Coca-Cola for example, are redefining capitalism along the principle of 'Shared Value', which involves creating economic value in a way that also creates value for society by addressing its needs and challenges. An example would be the Nestlé Company. Much criticised in earlier times, it now works closely with small farmers in impoverished parts of the world in redesigning its coffee procurement processes. The new approach involved Nestlé helping and supporting growers in a number of different ways: advice on farming best practice, assistance in securing stock fertilisers and pesticides, and introducing incentive schemes. From Nestlé's point of view they have been guaranteed a reliable supply of good quality coffee from a variety of different of geographical sources, and for the coffee growers incomes rose as coffee quality and yields grew, while the negative environmental impact of farms declined. This link between company profitability and corporate social responsibility is not philanthropy, and it is not redistribution. It is a concept that argues that the long-term sustainability and profitability of the business sector and the community within which it operates are mutually dependent.

'Shared Value' is now gaining real traction but it needs education within both the business and government sectors. In the recent World Economic Forum at Davos, the concept took centre stage when CEOs from around the globe discussed how their companies should take more responsibility for society's needs. It was reported that many, including Walmart and Unilever, actively advocated this broader approach. Interestingly, a PricewaterhouseCooper survey leading up to the conference concluded that for 76 per cent of CEOs surveyed, business was defined by more than financial profit, with more than 50 per cent advocating the creation of value for wider stakeholders as a key ingredient for long-term profitability. The shared value approach can redefine capitalism in terms of its long-term relationship to society's needs. Many argue that it can be the driver of both innovation and growth in the global economy as the focus shifts towards human needs, new markets, and the costs of social ills such as inequality. And finally, there is also the consideration that a purely financial view of work and life leaves much to be desired.

There are existential issues to do with purpose, with consequence, and with what will be handed on to future generations. An excessive focus on short-term profitability with disregard for the consequences for the community at large is ultimately a self-defeating approach.

In Ireland the government's approach is to raise money and then spend it in a way which is most likely to appeal to chosen sectors of the electorate. What is needed is a principles-driven vision, embracing people, the environment, education, health, and equality. Germany, which continues to suffer from its history of National Socialism and the Holocaust, offers a good example here. When the Berlin Wall came down the socialist experiment in East Germany was shown to have been a pathetic failure, at the same time oppressively interfering with people's lives and sorely mismanaging the economy.

The German government took the controversial and expensive step of seeking to integrate the East and West of the country as rapidly as possible, even to the point of legislating for parity between the respective currencies. This has turned out to be a phenomenal success story for both the country's prosperity and for its people. More recently the German Chancellor, Angela Merkel, is providing real humanitarian leadership in her supportive approach for millions of impoverished families fleeing from war-torn parts of the world. In the long-term I believe this will be a 'win-win' result for the European Union, and for Germany both for its reputation and in terms of the contribution which immigrants can make to the wealth and welfare of a country.

The shared value approach offers a genuine opportunity for Irish banks to take a leadership role in promoting a vision which can enhance their long-term profitability at the same time as providing real value to the broader community. Supporting entrepreneurship is one area which seems to make particular sense. The first requirement is for senior bank management to embrace the philosophy. Next, they must regularly communicate this to their staff. Such an engagement will need to be genuine and not just a public relations exercise.

Specifics might include the setting up of an appropriately resourced team within an individual bank to drive the philosophy of supporting entrepreneurship. And strategies might include mentoring programmes, the provision of equity, the facilitation of partnerships among SMEs, and engagement with the universities, and with schools from primary level upwards.

I have no illusions about the magnitude of the task in such and similar-type shared value initiatives. It will need imagination and resolve but the outcome over the longer term would handsomely justify the effort.

Epilogue

In April 2014 Keyna and I invited family and friends, more than a hundred people, to join us at the Fitzwilliam Lawn Tennis Club in celebration of our 50 years of marriage. I produced a 15-minute DVD of our years of married life which was shown at the party, and both Keyna and I spoke of our love for each other and our gratitude for friendship and good fortune in life. Our two sons Redmond and Dermot spoke eloquently and humorously, our grandchildren were all star turns and we engaged a really good jazz band to play until the early hours. There was an outpouring of warmth and affection for us from all our guests. It was a beautiful and somewhat surreal experience for us. We feel that this was a landmark event in our lives. One of our guests summed it up in a thank-you letter when he said, '*So often these events are full of false bonhomie; yours was the real deal*'.

Just a few months before, such a celebration would have seemed impossible as long-standing back problems had flared up early in 2014, causing me excruciating pain. The medical diagnosis back in 2013 had been: '*A compression of the spinal nerves by a combination of a prolapsed disc and overgrown bony spurs within the spinal canal, which together were causing compression of the nerve roots*'.

This sounds awful and at 75 years of age it was. I had been maltreating my back for a very long time. About thirty years earlier a medical consultant friend of mine told me that a day would come when my back would throw in the towel and short-term solutions like physiotherapy and the use of a brace would no longer suffice. The future was a long time away then, and I continued to regularly run on roads, to swing a golf club in stress-inducing ways and generally to pile the pressure on my lower back. And so it came to pass. For some time before this the back had started to rebel with some serious onslaughts of pain and a chronic restriction of movement. The first response was injections, preceded by an MRI scan designed to isolate the problem areas. In September 2013, I went into St Vincent's Private Hospital and had injections in the root of the sciatic nerve. This was only partially successful, and I soon had a recurrence of generalised back pain which encouraged the medics to give me four more back injections in late December.

Things settled down sufficiently to enable us to travel to our apartment in Tenerife in the New Year. This was to be a special holiday for us as 27 January was the date of our wedding 50 years previously. I had put some serious effort into finding a suitable hotel for this very special occasion, the five-star Hotel Botanica in Puerto de la Cruz was chosen and I booked several days in a suite. The best table at the best restaurant in Puerto de la Cruz was also reserved and the restaurant staffs were appropriately briefed about the importance of the occasion. It was all a smashing success, dining and wining, smooching and dancing, luxuriating in the spa and reminiscing, the works. God was good in allowing me to get through this special occasion with no back pain and stress free. The next day, however, was very different. Before heading back home to our apartment in Golf del Sur we took a short tour of Puerto de la Cruz and in particular its botanical gardens and lovely parks. While we were strolling through the gardens arm in arm, an awful pain struck my lower left side. The sciatic pain had returned with a vengeance, and it was so intense that I had to lie on the ground to get even a small amount of relief. I remember trying to move around, trying to find the least painful position, when you're in this sort of discomfort there is no embarrassment about having passers-by stare at you.

Thankfully we had paid our hotel account and put our luggage into the car so the immediate task was to get back to Golf del Sur as quickly as possible. The Excellent Medical Clinic is about 3 km from our apartment and this was our destination. The 40-minute journey back was torture; in all my experience of pain over the years this trapped sciatic nerve was the worst. It is powerful and relentless and you can't get at it. It's like a red-hot ball-bearing rolling around your insides. I had been to the Excellent Medical Clinic before and had been treated by Dr. Christina for a mild dose of pneumonia. I remembered Christina, who spoke passably good English, telling us that her family was still in Poland but that she was being well paid here and was able to send money home. I also fondly remembered her for having given me injections to clear up the pneumonia instead of the usual oral antibiotics. A major benefit of this was that I could continue to have a glass of wine during my holidays. Christina the munificent!

When we got to the clinic I was relieved to find that she was on duty. *'We will give you a strong pain killer by way of a drip. You must go home then and sleep and I will give you strong tablets in case the pain recurs, but my advice to you is get on a plane and go home as soon as you can and you should seek consultation with your back specialist'* she said.

I was put on an intravenous drip for an hour and sent home with a small packet of painkillers. I woke up in distress the next morning and took the prescribed medication. It had no effect. So, back to the clinic and Christina. She responded quickly.

'You must go immediately to the hospital clinic in Santa Cruz; I will give you a letter of introduction to the specialist and arrange for tests to be done. We do not have the facility for tests here. You go by ambulance, immediately; stop by your apartment only to pick up some belongings'.

An ancient ambulance arrived driven by an elderly Spanish man accompanied by a young lady with a beautiful smile, neither of whom spoke a word of English. It normally takes an hour to get to the capital city but they made it in 45 minutes. We were rocking and rolling most of the way in this antiquated ambulance but I don't recall any discomfort, probably because I had been given another dose of the 'special painkillers' at the Excellent Medical Clinic before we left.

'We speak your language' blazed the sign at Reception in the medical clinic in Santa Cruz. I took heart from this. Sadly, apart from the initial briefing with a young doctor and nurse, they most

definitely did not speak my language. I was to spend ten days in this clinic and communication (or the lack of it) was to become a major problem.

As one would expect in a hospital clinic there were regular meals and copious painkilling treatments, including intravenous drips, pills and injections, but despite repeated enquiries by Keyna there was no sign of any specialist. The painkillers were of little help and I had virtually stopped eating because I had to lie on my back all the time. In any event I had lost interest in food.

I had been admitted on Wednesday. It was not until Friday evening that Dr. Diego Martel, neurosurgeon, finally arrived on the scene. He had recently retired from the city's teaching hospital but he was quite a young looking man and clearly in fine fettle. Keyna looked him up later on Google and found that he was somewhat of a local celebrity, having competed for Spain in the 4 x 100 metre freestyle swimming in the 1968 Olympic Games in Mexico City. Initially he prescribed an MRI scan and he cajoled the staff in this unit to stay on a little later than normal on the Friday evening for this.

Realistically, I felt it would be Monday morning at the earliest before any scan results would be available but to my surprise a beaming Dr. Martel arrived in on Saturday morning to brief me on the situation. He was accompanied by his handsome wife who was to assist in the translating. She was also smiling broadly and seemed to welcome this opportunity to practise her linguistic skills.

'The news', he said through his interpreter, *'is not so good. The discs are in very bad condition, one of them will have to be removed, the canal through which the spinal cord passes will have to be enlarged and other discs will have to be reconstituted by adding a piece and screwing it into the bone'*.

He then took a piece of paper from his pocket and made a childish drawing on it to indicate what would be involved in the surgery. In his opinion there was some urgency in proceeding with the operation. He assured me he would have a first-class team with him; he expected the procedure would take approximately four and a half hours. The convalescent period would be measured in weeks. He told me that if I wished to have the operation at home arrangements could be made for a doctor to travel with me. However, my pain levels were so high that normal air travel was probably not a realistic proposition. There was no mention about the possibility of returning home by way of air ambulance at this stage.

All Sunday we debated the pros and cons of the consultant's advice. I also knew that by now Keyna would have talked with Redmond and Dermot, our two sons. By Monday morning the health insurers, who had been contacted when the problems started, advised us that they would only take responsibility for the operation being done in Tenerife if it was a case of life and death. If they were to pay for a four-hour operation locally they would need some time to establish the full costs of the operation and the hospital stay, and they made it quite clear that they would not be responsible for any further costs or complications that might arise as a result. For us, that did it. This was to be highly invasive surgery and I was appalled at the prospect of proceeding without suitable insurance cover for contingencies. The next day we had a further contact from the insurers to say that they were agreeable to my being taken home by an air ambulance but that this could only happen when there was confirmation of the availability of a hospital bed in Ireland and that an Irish neurosurgeon had agreed to take me under his care.

Enter my wonderful son, Dermot, a partner in a prominent Irish legal firm and through his connections with the firm's medical practice division he had an introduction to the senior physician at Dublin's Blackrock Clinic. When asked about my dilemma the physician reportedly said, *'If I had a problem like this in my family the man I would want to go to is Martin Murphy, a really top-class neurosurgeon'*. Mr. Murphy was attached to the Blackrock Hospital in a part-time capacity in addition to his sports consultancy practice. He agreed straight away to take me on and to reserve a hospital bed for me.

All of this took a great deal of time, and there was more to come, the hospital bed was contingent on there being a patient to avail of it immediately. The insurers for their part had been unwilling to make any enquiries about the cost and availability of an air ambulance until they knew that a hospital bed had been reserved. Unbelievably, it took until the end of the week for all of this to be resolved. Finally, on Saturday I got confirmation that the ambulance had been organised for the following Monday, when I would be picked up at the clinic at 9 a.m. By then I would have been ten days at the Tenerife clinic.

I was ecstatic about this information, this was by far the best outcome for me, and I knew that I would soon be in the safe hands of one of Dublin's top neurosurgeons and in one of Dublin's best hospitals.

Throughout all this the nursing staff did their best to be as pleasant and helpful to me as possible but communications continued to be a real problem. At times it became comic. The younger nurses were really keen to learn some English and saw me as a way to help them in this. On one occasion one of the nurses was doing a regular medical check (during which I was talking) when she interrupted with, *'Shut up your mouth'*, and then with a big smile said, *'You see, I learn some English, pretty good, eh'*?

I remember one night when my pain was extreme and sleep was impossible. I asked for a renewal of the intravenous drip only to be told that there were no more available in the clinic. This seemed unlikely; I can only put it down to another communications failure. And so it was a matter of staring at the ceiling and putting up with it for the night in the hope of some resolution the following day.

These ten days had been a great challenge for me, preoccupied as I was with pain and concern about the outcomes. With the help of the painkillers I was eventually able to move sufficiently to go to the bathroom and even eat some food, spoon-fed by Keyna. Conversation was a help but reading was out of the question, so I spent most of the time looking at the white walls and ceiling and thinking. Initially this process was random but in time it became much more structured and ultimately productive. I thought about my situation and how I was handling it, I thought about my life and all my good fortune, I thought about my philosophy of life. I recalled when I was very young listening to the great broadcaster, Eamonn Andrews, interviewing the painter Jack B. Yeats. Andrews was lavishly complimenting Yeats on his great art, when Yeats responded that his art was of little consequence and that what was really important was what he called *'The art of living'*.

This is the real challenge for us all and to meet it we need self-knowledge, a knowledge of our unique individual talent and potential, and a willingness to work on nurturing these talents in lifelong learning. Carl Jung, the great psychoanalyst and philosopher, used to talk about what he called *'individuation'*: becoming one's own self through the process of self-realisation. I have always felt comfortable with Jung's approach to life as continuous self-development, and his notion that the journey which we call life is acceptance of ourselves in an eternal now.

As I lay in a hospital bed in Santa Cruz, Tenerife's capital city, I reflected on my eventful life over the past 75 years: of my great good fortune in meeting and marrying Keyna more than fifty years ago, of our sons, our daughters-in-law and our five grandchildren, of all the breaks I got and all the opportunities afforded me to develop and grow. I thought about my somewhat callow and certainly lazy youth and the early days as a junior bank clerk in the Hibernian Bank. Jung wrote about success in the first half of life as often demanding the development of a one-sided approach to reality and the channelling of energy in one highly specific direction. Over the years, he held, this can result in a serious '*Diminution of personality, with much self-potential falling into the unconscious*'. Not having achieved any great success in the early part of my life this hardly applies to me. Jung's advice is that what is needed is an inner stock-taking of what has been achieved and what has been missed and therefore what remains to be fulfilled. This, he said, was part of the mid-life transition and a very real step towards self-individuation.

Monday morning dawned and at 9 am I was given another dose of intravenous painkillers. Then I was taken down by stretcher to the waiting ambulance to be transported to the air ambulance and from there straight home to Dublin. Of course, it was not to be as simple as that. The winds were particularly high that day and it was not possible to leave by the nearer airport in the northern part of Tenerife, so the ambulance had to go to the southern airport, a journey of 60 km. There was an interminable delay at the airport, and then I was told that we were to be diverted to Lanzarote where the plan was to refuel and pick up another sick passenger. Another long delay at Lanzarote and finally we were airborne and on our way to Dublin. The air ambulance was a Lear jet, built like a capsule, with very little headroom and with baggage strewn all over the floor. This narrow space was a problem for me as I am somewhat claustrophobic, probably arising from my boyhood experience of nearly being trapped in a tunnel which, according to legend, had been used as a 'priests' escape' in the penal times in Ireland, as mentioned earlier.

The on-board arrangement was supposed to be that a doctor would be in attendance but there was no doctor, only a very jolly nurse, two pilots and a couple of others whose purpose was unclear to me. I don't recall being offered any food or water throughout the flight, although I assume that this was because I was either sleeping or pretending to be asleep. Amazingly, the pain levels were bearable throughout the journey.

The normal flight from Tenerife to Dublin is about four and a quarter hours; mine took ten hours, including all the delays such as the stopover at Lanzarote and a further stopover and more refuelling at Shannon airport.

We reached Dublin Airport about 7.30 in the evening and I arrived at the Blackrock Clinic at 8.30. I was stretchered into the foyer of the hospital and I cannot describe the beautiful sight of my two sons and my lovely wife who were there to greet me.

During my ten days in the clinic and on the journey back to Dublin, I thought about falling in love with Keyna, my soul-mate and the great influence on my search for meaning and goals in my life. I would never have opted to enrol as a night student in the Commerce faculty of UCD back in 1964 without her encouragement and support and not least the £50 to pay college tuition fees which came from Keyna's working throughout the summer at correcting Leaving Certificate examination papers in

Home Economics. This, we both believe, was the start which led to so much bounty in later years.

I reflected on the torrent of life happenings which seemed to flow from this first step. I thought about my Harvard days, about the early years with the Bank of Ireland's overseas department; I thought about the opportunity to start a new bank and the people I worked with in this happy endeavour; and I thought about my years working with Belvedere College and the Jesuits. I thought about going on a mission for the IMF to the Central Bank in the Czech Republic, expecting to be joined by two senior public servants from other European countries and discovering when I arrived in Prague that I was on my own; and I thought about the opportunity to be involved as chairman in one of Hungary's top banks in the early privatisation years. Mostly it was not a question of reflecting on events and achievements, rather on the privilege of being there and of the people I met.

If I ever get out of here, I thought, I should seriously consider writing the story of this journey. And now I have done so.

Index

University College, Dublin 66,
71, 74, 196

University College, Galway 44

Ustinov, Peter 136, 137

Vermiren, Remi 206, 222, 229

Virginia, County Cavan 34

Walmart Company 275

Walsh, Prof. Noel 235, 236

Wauters, Prof. Luc 144, 145,
171

Welles, Orson 45

Whitaker, T.K. 30

White, Pat 63

Wilkinson, Sir Neville 14

Williams and Glyn's Bank 110

Wilson, Brian 200, 202, 244

Wilson, Geoffrey 128, 129

Winter, Claude and Catherine
136, 137

Withofs, Cornil 154, 155, 182

Wogan, Sir Terry 18, 19

Woodward, Joanne *The Three
Faces of Eve* 50

Woosnam, Ian 234

World Bank 200, 201, 205

World Economic Forum in
Davos (2015) 265

Wright, Paddy 190

Wriston, Walter 98, 120

Yeats, Jack B. 286

Young, Nancy 165